UNWIN PAPERBACKS

Sceptical Essays

'Into every tidy scheme for arranging the pattern of human life, it is necessary to inject a certain dose of anarchism – enough to prevent immobility leading to decay, but not enough to bring about disruption.'

With these words Bertrand Russell concludes his *Sceptical Essays*, a magnificent *jeu d'esprit* (albeit a deadly serious one) in which he examines the attitudes and prejudices of the twentieth century. Science, psychology, philosophy, Eastern and Western ideas of happiness, behaviourism, puritanism, socialism, Freud, Christ, Marx and Buddha all come under Russell's sceptical gaze and none escape without a flick, if not a lash, from his critical tongue.

Written with wit as well as candour, these essays reflect what Russell saw as his prime role – to challenge, to question, and to debate.

Sceptical Essays

BERTRAND RUSSELL

UNWIN PAPERBACKS

First published in October 1935
Second impression November 1935
Third impression January 1936
Fourth impression 1948
Fifth impression 1952
Sixth impression 1955
First published in Unwin Books 1960
Second impression 1961
Third impression 1962
Fourth impression 1963
Fifth impression 1966
Sixth impression 1970
First published in Unwin Paperbacks 1977

ISBN 0 04 104003 1

UNWIN PAPERBACKS
George Allen & Unwin (Publishers) Ltd
Ruskin House, Museum Street
London WC1A 1LU

Printed in Great Britain
in 10 on 10$\frac{1}{2}$ pt Plantin
by Cox & Wyman Ltd,
London, Reading and Fakenham

Aimer et penser: c'est la veritable
vie des esprits.

VOLTAIRE

Contents

Chapter 1

Introduction: On the Value of Scepticism

I wish to propose for the reader's favourable consideration a doctrine which may, I fear, appear wildly paradoxical and subversive. The doctrine in question is this: that it is undesirable to believe a proposition when there is no ground whatever for supposing it true. I must, of course, admit that if such an opinion became common it would completely transform our social life and our political system; since both are at present faultless, this must weigh against it. I am also aware (what is more serious) that it would tend to diminish the incomes of clairvoyants, bookmakers, bishops and others who live on the irrational hopes of those who have done nothing to deserve good fortune here or hereafter. In spite of these grave arguments, I maintain that a case can be made out for my paradox, and I shall try to set it forth.

First of all, I wish to guard myself against being thought to take up an extreme position. I am a British Whig, with a British love of compromise and moderation. A story is told of Pyrrho, the founder of Pyrrhonism (which was the old name for scepticism). He maintained that we never know enough to be sure that one course of action is wiser than another. In his youth, when he was taking his constitutional one afternoon, he saw his teacher in philosophy (from whom he had imbibed his principles) with his head stuck in a ditch, unable to get out. After contemplating him for some time, he walked on, maintaining that there was no sufficient ground for thinking he would do any good by pulling the old man out. Others, less sceptical, effected a rescue, and blamed Pyrrho for his heartlessness. But his teacher, true to his principles, praised him for his consistency. Now I do not advocate such heroic scepticism as that. I am prepared to admit the ordinary beliefs of common sense, in practice if not in theory. I am prepared to admit any well-established result of science, not as certainly true, but as sufficiently probable to afford a basis for rational action. If it is announced that there is to be an eclipse of the moon on such-and-such a date, I think it worthwhile to look and see whether it is taking place. Pyrrho would have thought otherwise. On this ground, I feel justified in claiming that I advocate a middle position.

There are matters about which those who have investigated them are agreed; the dates of eclipses may serve as an illustration. There are other matters about which experts are not agreed. Even when the experts all agree, they may well be mistaken. Einstein's view as to the magnitude of the deflection of light by gravitation would have been rejected by all experts twenty years ago, yet it proved to be right. Nevertheless the opinion of experts, when it is unanimous, must be accepted by non-experts as more likely to be right than the opposite opinion. The scepticism that I advocate amounts only to this: (1) that when the experts are agreed, the opposite opinion cannot be held to be certain; (2) that when they are not agreed, no opinion can be regarded as certain by a non-expert; and (3) that when they all hold that no sufficient grounds for a positive opinion exist, the ordinary man would do well to suspend his judgement.

These propositions may seem mild, yet, if accepted, they would absolutely revolutionise human life.

The opinions for which people are willing to fight and persecute all belong to one of the three classes which this scepticism condemns. When there are rational grounds for an opinion, people are content to set them forth and wait for them to operate. In such cases, people do not hold their opinions with passion; they hold them calmly, and set forth their reasons quietly. The opinions that are held with passion are always those for which no good ground exists; indeed the passion is the measure of the holder's lack of rational conviction. Opinions in politics and religion are almost always held passionately. Except in China, a man is thought a poor creature unless he has strong opinions on such matters; people hate sceptics far more than they hate the passionate advocates of opinions hostile to their own. It is thought that the claims of practical life demand opinions on such questions, and that, if we became more rational, social existence would be impossible. I believe the opposite of this, and will try to make it clear why I have this belief.

Take the question of unemployment in the years after 1920.

One party held that it was due to the wickedness of trade unions, another that it was due to the confusion on the Continent. A third party, while admitting that these causes played a part, attributed most of the trouble to the policy of the Bank of England in trying to increase the value of the pound sterling. This third party, I am given to understand, contained most of the experts, but no one else. Politicians do not find any attractions in a view which does not lend itself to party declamation, and ordinary mortals prefer views which attribute misfortune to the machinations of their enemies. Consequently people fight for and against quite irrelevant measures, while the few who have a rational opinion are not listened to because they do not minister to any one's passions. To produce converts, it would have been necessary to persuade people that the Bank of England is wicked. To convert Labour, it would have been necessary to show that directors of the Bank of England are hostile to trade unionism; to convert the Bishop of London, it would have been necessary to show that they are 'immoral'. It would be thought to follow that their views on currency are mistaken.

Let us take another illustration. It is often said that socialism is contrary to human nature, and this assertion is denied by socialists with the same heat with which it is made by their opponents. The late Dr Rivers, whose death cannot be sufficiently deplored, discussed this question in a lecture at University College, published in his posthumous book on *Psychology and Politics*. This is the only discussion of this topic known to me that can lay claim to be scientific. It sets forth certain anthropological data which show that socialism is not contrary to human nature in Melanesia; it then points out that we do not know whether human nature is the same in Melanesia as in Europe; and it concludes that the only way of finding out whether socialism is contrary to European human nature is to try it. It is interesting that on the basis of this conclusion he was willing to become a Labour candidate. But he would certainly not have added to the heat and passion in which political controversies are usually enveloped.

I will now venture on a topic which people find even more difficulty in treating dispassionately, namely marriage customs. The bulk of the population of every country is persuaded that all marriage customs other than its own are immoral, and that those who combat this view only do so in order to justify their own loose lives. In India, the re-marriage of widows is traditionally regarded as a thing too horrible to contemplate. In Catholic countries, divorce is thought very wicked, but some failure of conjugal fidelity is tolerated, at least in men. In America, divorce is easy, but extra-conjugal relations are condemned with the utmost severity. Mohammedans believe in polygamy, which we think degrading. All these differing opinions are held with extreme vehemence, and very cruel persecutions are inflicted upon those who contravene them. Yet no one in any of the various countries makes the slightest attempt to show that the custom of his own country contributes more to human happiness than the custom of others.

When we open any scientific treatise on the subject, such as (for example) Westermarck's *History of Human Marriage*, we find an atmosphere extraordinarily different from that of popular prejudice. We find that every kind of custom has existed, many of them such as we should have supposed repugnant to human nature. We think we can understand polygamy, as a custom forced upon women by male oppressors. But what are we to say of the Tibetan custom, according to which one woman has several husbands? Yet travellers in Tibet assure us that family life there is at least as harmonious as in Europe. A little of such reading must soon reduce any candid person to complete scepticism, since there seem to be no data enabling us to say that one marriage custom is better or worse than another. Almost all involve cruelty and intolerance toward offenders against the local code, but otherwise they have nothing in common. It seems that sin is geographical. From this conclusion, it is only a small step to the further conclusion that the notion of 'sin' is illusory, and that the cruelty habitually practised in punishing it is unnecessary. It is just this conclusion which is so unwelcome to many minds, since the infliction of cruelty with a good conscience is a delight to moralists. That is why they invented Hell.

Nationalism is of course an extreme example of fervent belief concerning doubtful matters. I think it may be safely said that any scientific historian, writing now a history of the Great War, is bound to make statements which, if made during the war, would have exposed him to imprisonment in every one of the belligerent countries on both sides. Again with the exception of China, there is no country where people tolerate the truth about themselves; at ordinary times, the truth is only thought ill-mannered, but in wartime it is thought criminal. Opposing systems of violent belief are built up, the falsehood of which is evident from the fact that they are only believed by those who share the same national bias. But the application of reason to these systems of belief is thought as wicked as the application of reason to religious dogmas was formerly thought. When people are challenged as to why scepticism in such matters should be wicked, the only answer is that myths help to win wars, so that a rational nation would be killed rather than kill. The view that there is something shameful in saving one's skin by wholesale slander of foreigners is one which, so far as I know, has hitherto found no supporters among professional moralists outside the ranks of the Quakers. If it is suggested that a rational nation would find ways of keeping out of wars altogether, the answer is usually mere abuse.

What would be the effect of a spread of rational scepticism? Human events spring from passions, which generate systems of attendant myths. Psycho-analysts have studied the individual manifestations of this process in lunatics, certified and uncertified. A man who has suffered some humiliation invents a theory that he is King of England, and develops all kinds of ingenious explanations of the fact that he is not treated with that respect which his exalted position demands. In this case, his delusion is one with which his neighbours do not sympathise, so they lock him up. But if, instead of asserting only his own greatness, he asserts the greatness of his nation or his class or his creed, he wins hosts of adherents, and becomes a political or religious leader, even if, to the impartial outsider, his views seem just as absurd as those found in asylums. In this way a collective insanity grows up, which follows laws very similar to those of individual insanity. Every one knows that it is dangerous to dispute with a lunatic who thinks he is King of England; but as he is isolated, he can be overpowered. When a whole nation shares a delusion, its anger is of the same kind as that of an individual lunatic if its pretensions are disputed, but nothing short of war can compel it to submit to reason.

The part played by intellectual factors in human behaviour is a matter as to which there is much disagreement among psychologists. There are two quite distinct questions: (1) how far are beliefs operative as causes of actions? (2) how far are beliefs derived from logically adequate evidence, or capable of being so derived? On both questions, psychologists are agreed in giving a much smaller place to the intellectual factors than the plain man would give, but within this general agreement there is room for considerable differences of degree. Let us take the two questions in succession.

(1) How far are beliefs operative as causes of action? Let us not discuss the question theoretically, but let us take an ordinary day of an ordinary man's life. He begins by getting up in the morning, probably from force of habit, without the intervention of any belief. He eats his breakfast, catches his train, reads his newspaper, and goes to his office, all from force of habit. There was a time in the past when he formed these habits, and in the choice of the office, at least, belief played a part. He probably believed, at the time, that the job offered him there was as good as he was likely to get. In most men, belief plays a part in the original choice of a career, and therefore, derivatively, in all that is entailed by this choice.

At the office, if he is an underling, he may continue to act merely from habit, without active volition, and without the explicit intervention of belief. It might be thought that, if he adds up columns of figures, he believes the arithmetical rules which he employs. But that would be an error; these rules are mere habits of his body, like those of a tennis player. They were acquired in youth, not from an intellectual belief that they corresponded to the truth, but to please the schoolmaster, just as a dog learns to sit on its hind legs and beg for food. I do not say that all education is of this sort, but certainly most learning of the three R's is.

If, however, our friend is a partner or director, he may be called upon during his day to make difficult decisions of policy. In these decisions it is probable that belief will play a part. He believes that some things will go up and others will go down, that so-and-so is a sound man, and such-and-such on the verge of bankruptcy. On these beliefs he acts. It is just because he is called upon to act on beliefs rather than mere habits that he is considered such a much greater man than a mere clerk, and is able to get so much more money – provided his beliefs are true.

In his home-life there will be much the same proportion of occasions when belief is a cause of action. At ordinary times, his behaviour to his wife and children will be governed by habit, or by instinct modified by habit. On great occasions – when he proposes marriage, when he decides what school to send his son to, or when he finds reason to suspect his wife of unfaithfulness – he cannot be guided wholly by habit. In proposing marriage he may be guided by mere instinct, or he may be influenced by the belief that the lady is rich. If he is guided by instinct, he no doubt believes that the lady possesses every virtue, and this may seem to him to be a cause of his action, but in fact it is merely another effect of the instinct which alone suffices to account for his action. In choosing a school for his son, he probably proceeds in much the same way as in making difficult business decisions; here belief usually plays an important part. If evidence comes into his possession showing that his wife has been unfaithful, his behaviour is likely to be purely instinctive, but the instinct is set in operation by a belief, which is the first cause of everything that follows.

Thus although beliefs are not directly responsible for more than a small part of our actions, the actions for which they are responsible are among the most important, and largely determine the general structure of our lives. In particular, our religious and political actions are associated with beliefs.

(2) I come now to our second question, which is itself twofold: (a) how far are beliefs in fact based upon evidence? (b) how far is it possible or desirable that they should be?

(a) The extent to which beliefs are based upon evidence is very much less than believers suppose. Take the kind of action which is most nearly rational: the investment of money by a rich City man. You will often find that his view (say) on the question whether the French franc will go up or down depends upon his political sympathies, and yet is so strongly held that he is prepared to risk money on it. In bankruptcies it often appears that some sentimental factor was the original cause of ruin. Political opinions are hardly ever based upon evidence, except in the case of civil servants, who are forbidden to give utterance to them. There are of course exceptions. In the tariff reform controversy which began twenty-five years ago, most manufacturers supported the side that would increase their own incomes, showing that their opinions were really based on evidence, however little their utterances would have led one to suppose so. We have here a complication. Freudians have accustomed us to 'rationalising', i.e. the process of inventing what seem to ourselves rational grounds for a decision or opinion that is in fact quite irrational. But there is, especially in

English-speaking countries, a converse process which may be called 'irrationalising'. A shrewd man will sum up, more or less subconsciously, the pros and cons of a question from a selfish point of view. (Unselfish considerations seldom weigh subconsciously except where one's children are concerned.) Having come to a sound egoistic decision by the help of the unconscious, a man proceeds to invent, or adopt from others, a set of high-sounding phrases showing how he is pursuing the public good at immense personal sacrifice. Anybody who believes that these phrases give his real reasons must suppose him quite incapable of judging evidence, since the supposed public good is not going to result from his action. In this case a man appears less rational than he is; what is still more curious, the irrational part of him is conscious and the rational part unconscious. It is this trait in our characters that has made the English and Americans so successful.

Shrewdness, when it is genuine, belongs more to the unconscious than to the conscious part of our nature. It is, I suppose, the main quality required for success in business. From a moral point of view, it is a humble quality, since it is always selfish; yet it suffices to keep men from the worst crimes. If the Germans had had it, they would not have adopted the unlimited submarine campaign. If the French had had it, they would not have behaved as they did in the Ruhr. If Napoleon had had it, he would not have gone to war again after the Treaty of Amiens. It may be laid down as a general rule to which there are few exceptions that, when people are mistaken as to what is to their own interest, the course that they believe to be wise is more harmful to others than the course that really is wise. Therefore anything that makes people better judges of their own interest does good. There are innumerable examples of men making fortunes because, on moral grounds, they did something which they believed to be contrary to their own interests. For instance, among early Quakers there were a number of shopkeepers who adopted the practice of asking no more for their goods than they were willing to accept, instead of bargaining with each customer, as everybody else did. They adopted this practice because they held it to be a lie to ask more than they would take. But the convenience to customers was so great that everybody came to their shops, and they grew rich. (I forget where I read this, but if my memory serves me it was in some reliable source.) The same policy *might* have been adopted from shrewdness, but in fact no one was sufficiently shrewd. Our unconscious is more malevolent than it pays us to be; therefore the people who do most completely what is in fact to their interest are those who deliberately, on moral grounds, do what they believe to be against their interest. Next to them come the people who try to think out rationally and consciously what is to their own interest, eliminating as far as possible the influence of passion. Third come the people who have instinctive shrewdness. Last of all come the people whose malevolence overbalances their shrewdness, making them pursue the ruin of others in ways that lead to their own ruin. This last class embraces 90 per cent of the population of Europe.

I may seem to have digressed somewhat from my topic, but it was necessary to disentangle unconscious reason, which is called shrewdness, from the conscious variety. The ordinary methods of education have practically no effect upon the unconscious, so that shrewdness cannot be taught by our present technique. Morality, also, except where it consists of mere habit, seems incapable of being taught by present methods; at any rate I have never noticed any beneficent effect upon those who are exposed to frequent exhortations. Therefore on our present lines any deliberate improvement must be brought about by intellectual means. We do not know how to teach people to be shrewd or virtuous, but we do know, within limits, how to teach them to be rational: it is only necessary to reverse the practice of education authorities in every particular. We may hereafter learn to create virtue by manipulating the ductless glands and stimulating or restraining their secretions. But for the present it is easier to create rationality than virtue – meaning by 'rationality' a scientific habit of mind in forecasting the effects of our actions.

(b) This brings me to the question: How far could or should men's actions be rational? Let us take 'should' first. There are very definite limits, to my mind, within which rationality should be confined; some of the most important departments of life are ruined by the invasion of reason. Leibniz in his old age told a correspondent that he had only once asked a lady to marry him, and that was when he was fifty. 'Fortunately,' he added, 'the lady asked time to consider. This gave me also time to consider, and I withdrew the offer.' Doubtless his conduct was very rational, but I cannot say that I admire it.

Shakespeare puts 'the lunatic, the lover, and the poet' together, as being 'of imagination all compact'. The problem is to keep the lover and the poet, without the lunatic. I will give an illustration. In 1919 I saw *The Trojan Women* acted at the Old Vic. There is an unbearably pathetic scene where Astyanax is put to death by the Greeks for fear he should grow up into a second Hector. There was hardly a dry eye in the theatre, and the audience found the cruelty of the Greeks in the play hardly credible. Yet those very people who wept were, at that very moment, practising that very cruelty on a scale which the imagination of Euripides could have never contemplated. They had lately voted (most of them) for a Government which prolonged the blockade of Germany after the armistice, and imposed the blockade of Russia. It was known that these blockades caused the death of immense numbers of children, but it was felt desirable to diminish the population of enemy countries: the children, like Astyanax, might grow up to emulate their fathers. Euripides the poet awakened the lover in the imagination of the audience; but lover and poet were forgotten at the door of the theatre, and the lunatic (in the shape of the homicidal maniac) controlled the political actions of these men and women who thought themselves kind and virtuous.

Is it possible to preserve the lover and the poet without preserving the lunatic? In each of us, all three exist in varying degrees. Are they so bound up together that when the one is brought under control the others perish? I do not believe it. I believe that there is in each of us a certain energy which must find vent in actions not inspired by reason, but may find vent in art, in passionate love, or in passionate hate, according to circumstances. Respectability, regularity and routine – the whole cast-iron discipline of a modern industrial society – have atrophied the artistic impulse, and imprisoned love so that it can no longer be generous and free and creative, but must be either stuffy or furtive. Control has been applied to the very things which should be free, while envy, cruelty and hate sprawl at large with the blessing of nearly the whole bench of Bishops. Our instinctive apparatus consists of two parts – the one tending to further our own life and that of our descendants, the other tending to thwart the lives of supposed rivals. The first includes the joy of life, and love, and art, which is psychologically an offshoot of love. The second includes competition, patriotism and war. Conventional morality does everything to suppress the first and encourage the second. True morality would do the exact opposite. Our dealings with those whom we love may be safely left to instinct; it is our dealings with those whom we hate that ought to be brought under the dominion of reason. In the modern world, those whom we effectively hate are distant groups, especially foreign nations. We conceive them abstractly, and deceive ourselves into the belief that acts which are really embodiments of hatred are done from love of justice or some such lofty motive. Only a large measure of scepticism can tear away the veils which hide this truth from us. Having achieved that, we could begin to build a new morality, not based on envy and restriction, but on the wish for a full life and the realisation that other human beings are a help and not a hindrance when once the madness of envy has been cured. This is not a Utopian hope; it was partially realised in Elizabethan England. It could be realised tomorrow if men would learn to pursue their own happiness rather than the misery of others. This is no impossibly austere morality yet its adoption would turn our earth into a paradise.

Chapter 2

Dreams and Facts

I

The influence of our wishes upon our beliefs is a matter of
common knowledge and observation, yet the nature of this
influence is very generally misconceived. It is customary to suppose that the bulk of our beliefs are derived from some rational
ground, and that desire is only an occasional disturbing force. The
exact opposite of this would be nearer the truth: the great mass of
beliefs by which we are supported in our daily life is merely the
bodying forth of desire, corrected here and there, at isolated
points, by the rude shock of fact. Man is essentially a dreamer,
wakened sometimes for a moment by some peculiarly obtrusive
element in the outer world, but lapsing again quickly into the
happy somnolence of imagination. Freud has shown how largely
our dreams at night are the pictured fulfilment of our wishes;
he has, with an equal measure of truth, said the same of day-
dreams; and he might have included the day-dreams which we
call beliefs.

There are three ways by which this non-rational origin of our
convictions can be demonstrated: there is the way of psycho-
analysis, which, starting from an understanding of the insane and
the hysterical, gradually makes it plain how little, in essence, these
victims of malady differ from ordinary healthy people; then there
is the way of the sceptical philosopher, showing how feeble is the
rational evidence for even our most cherished beliefs; and finally
there is the way of common observation of men. It is only the last
of these three that I propose to consider.

The lowest savages, as they have become known through the
labours of anthropologists, are not found groping in conscious ignorance amid phenomena that they are aware of not understanding. On the contrary, they have innumerable beliefs, so
firmly held as to control all their more important actions. They

believe that by eating the flesh of an animal or a warrior it is possible to acquire the virtues possessed by the victim when alive. Many of them believe that to pronounce the name of their chief is such sacrilege as to bring instant death; they even go so far as to alter all words in which his name occurs as one of the syllables; for example, if we had a king named John, we should speak of a jonquil as (say) a George-quil, and of a dungeon as a dun-george. When they advance to agriculture, and weather becomes important for the food supply, they believe that magical incantations or the kindling of small fires will cause rain to come or the sun to burn brightly. They believe that when a man is slain his blood, or ghost, pursues the slayer to obtain vengeance, but can be misled by a simple disguise such as painting the face red or putting on mourning.[1] The first half of this belief has obviously originated from those who feared murder, the second from those who had committed it.

Nor are irrational beliefs confined to savages. A great majority of the human race have religious opinions different from our own, and therefore groundless. People interested in politics, with the exception of politicians, have passionate convictions upon innumerable questions which must appear incapable of rational decision to any unprejudiced person. Voluntary workers in a contested election always believe that their side will win, no matter what reason there may be for expecting defeat. There can be no doubt that, in the autumn of 1914, the immense majority of the German nation felt absolutely certain of victory for Germany. In this case fact has intruded and dispelled the dream. But if, by some means, all non-German historians could be prevented from writing during the next hundred years, the dream would reinstate itself: the early triumphs would be remembered, while the ultimate disaster would be forgotten.

Politeness is the practice of respecting that part of a man's beliefs which is specially concerned with his own merits or those of his group. Every man, wherever he goes, is encompassed by a cloud of comforting convictions, which move with him like flies on a summer day. Some of these convictions are personal to himself: they tell him of his virtues and excellencies, the affection of his friends and the respect of his acquaintances, the rosy prospect of

[1] See the chapter on 'The Mark of Cain' in Frazer's *Folk-lore in the Old Testament*.

his career, and his unflagging energy in spite of delicate health. Next come convictions of the superior excellence of his family: how his father had that unbending rectitude which is now so rare, and brought up his children with a strictness beyond what is to be found among modern parents; how his sons are carrying all before them in school games, and his daughter is not the sort of girl to make an imprudent marriage. Then there are beliefs about his class, which, according to his station, is the best socially, or the most intelligent, or the most deserving morally, of the classes in the community – though all are agreed that the first of these merits is more desirable than the second, and the second than the third. Concerning his nation, also, almost every man cherishes comfortable delusions. 'Foreign nations, I am sorry to say, do as they do do.' So said Mr Podsnap, giving expression, in these words, to one of the deepest sentiments of the human heart. Finally we come to the theories that exalt mankind in general, either absolutely or in comparison with the 'brute creation'. Men have souls, though animals have not; Man is the 'rational animal'; any peculiarly cruel or unnatural action is called 'brutal' or 'bestial' (although such actions are in fact distinctively human)[1]; God made Man in His own image, and the welfare of Man is the ultimate purpose of the universe.

We have thus a hierarchy of comforting beliefs: those private to the individual, those which he shares with his family, those common to his class or his nation, and finally those that are equally delightful to all mankind. If we desire good relations with a man, we must respect these beliefs; we do not, therefore, speak of a man to his face as we should behind his back. The difference increases as his remoteness from our selves grows greater. In speaking to a brother, we have no need of conscious politeness as regards his parents. The need of politeness is at its maximum in speaking with foreigners, and is so irksome as to be paralysing to those who are only accustomed to compatriots. I remember once suggesting to an untravelled American that possibly there were a few small points in which the British Constitution compared favourably with that of the United States. He instantly fell into a towering passion; having never heard such an opinion before, he could not imagine that anyone seriously entertained it. We had both failed in politeness, and the result was disaster.

[1] Compare Mark Twain's *Mysterious Stranger*.

But the results of failure in politeness, however bad from the point of view of a social occasion, are admirable from the point of view of dispelling myths. There are two ways in which our natural beliefs are corrected: one the contact with fact, as when we mistake a poisonous fungus for a mushroom and suffer pain in consequence; the other, when our beliefs conflict, not directly with objective fact, but with the opposite beliefs of other men. One man thinks it lawful to eat pork, but not beef; another, beef but not pork. The usual result of this difference of opinion has been bloodshed; but gradually there is beginning to be a rationalist opinion that perhaps neither is really sinful. Modesty, the correlative of politeness, consists in pretending not to think better of ourselves and our belongings than of the man we are speaking to and his belongings. It is only in China that this art is thoroughly understood. I am told that, if you ask a Chinese mandarin after the health of his wife and children, he will reply: 'That contemptible slut and her verminous brood are, as your Magnificence deigns to be informed, in the enjoyment of rude health.'[1] But such elaboration demands a dignified and leisurely existence; it is impossible in the swift but important contacts of business or politics. Step by step, relations with other human beings dispel the myths of all but the most successful. Personal conceit is dispelled by brothers, family conceit by schoolfellows, class conceit by politics, national conceit by defeat in war or commerce. But human conceit remains, and in this region, so far as the effect of social intercourse is concerned, the myth-making faculty has free play. Against this form of delusion, a partial corrective is found in Science; but the corrective can never be more than partial, for without some credulity Science itself would crumble and collapse.

II

Men's personal and group dreams may be ludicrous, but their collective human dreams, to us who cannot pass outside the circle of humanity, are pathetic. The universe as astronomy reveals it is very vast. How much there may be beyond what our telescopes show, we cannot tell; but what we can know is of unimaginable

[1] This was written before I came to know China. It would not be true of the China that I saw (in 1920).

immensity. In the visible world, the Milky Way is a tiny fragment; within this fragment, the solar system is an infinitesimal
speck, and of this speck our planet is a microscopic dot. On this
dot, tiny lumps of impure carbon and water, of complicated structure, with somewhat unusual physical and chemical properties,
crawl about for a few years, until they are dissolved again into the
elements of which they are compounded. They divide their time
between labour designed to postpone the moment of dissolution
for themselves and frantic struggles to hasten it for others of their
kind. Natural convulsions periodically destroy some thousands or
millions of them, and disease prematurely sweeps away many
more. These events are considered to be misfortunes; but when
men succeed in inflicting similar destruction by their own efforts,
they rejoice, and give thanks to God. In the life of the solar
system, the period during which the existence of man will have
been physically possible is a minute portion of the whole; but
there is some reason to hope that even before this period is ended
man will have set a term to his own existence by his efforts at
mutual annihilation. Such is man's life viewed from the outside.

But such a view of life, we are told, is intolerable, and would
destroy the instinctive energy by which men persist. The way of
escape that they have found is through religion and philosophy.
However alien and indifferent the outer world may seem, we are
assured by our comforters that there is harmony beneath the apparent conflict. All the long development from the original nebula
is supposed to lead up to man as the culmination of the process.
Hamlet is a very well-known play, yet few readers would have any
recollection of the part of the First Sailor, which consists of the
four words: 'God bless you, sir.' But suppose a society of men
whose sole business in life was to act this part; suppose them
isolated from contact with the Hamlets, Horatios and even Guild-
ensterns: would they not invent systems of literary criticism according to which the four words of the First Sailor were the kernel
of the whole drama? Would they not punish with ignominy or
exile any one of their number who should suggest that other parts
were possibly of equal importance? And the life of mankind takes
up a much smaller proportion of the universe than the First
Sailor's speech does of *Hamlet*, but we cannot listen behind the
scenes to the rest of the play, and we know very little of its characters or plot.

When we think of mankind, we think primarily of ourself as its representative; we therefore think well of mankind, and consider its preservation important. Mr Jones, the Nonconformist grocer, is sure that he deserves eternal life, and that a universe which refused it to him would be intolerably bad. But when he thinks of Mr Robinson, his Anglican competitor, who mixes sand with his sugar and is lax about Sunday, he feels that the universe might well carry charity too far. To complete his happiness, there is need of hell-fire for Mr Robinson; in this way, the cosmic importance of man is preserved, but the vital distinction between friends and enemies is not obliterated by a weak universal benevolence. Mr Robinson holds the same view with the parts inverted, and general happiness results.

In the days before Copernicus there was no need of philosophic subtlety to maintain the anthropocentric view of the world. The heavens visibly revolved about the earth, and on the earth man had dominion over all the beasts of the field. But when the earth lost its central position, man, too, was deposed from his eminence, and it became necessary to invent a metaphysic to correct the 'crudities' of science. This task was achieved by those who are called 'idealists', who maintain that the world of matter is unreal appearance, while the reality is Mind or Spirit – transcending the mind or spirit of the philosopher as he transcends common men. So far from there being no place like home, these thinkers assure us that every place is like home. In all our best, that is, in all those tasks which we share with the philosopher in question, we are at one with the universe. Hegel assures us that the universe resembles the Prussian State of his day; his English followers consider it more analogous to a bi-cameral plutocratic democracy. The reasons offered for these views are carefully camouflaged so as to conceal even from their authors the connection with human wishes: they are derived, nominally, from such dry sources as logic and the analysis of propositions. But the influence of wishes is shown by the fallacies committed, which all tend in one direction. When a man adds up an account, he is much more likely to make a mistake in his favour than to his detriment; and when a man reasons, he is more apt to incur fallacies which favour his wishes than such as thwart them. And so it comes that, in the study of nominally abstract thinkers, it is their mistakes that give the key to their personality.

Many may contend that, even if the systems men have invented are untrue, they are harmless and comforting, and should be left undisturbed. But they are in fact not harmless, and the comfort they bring is dearly bought by the preventable misery which they lead men to tolerate. The evils of life spring partly from natural causes, partly from men's hostility to each other. In former times, competition and war were necessary for the securing of food, which could only be obtained by the victors. Now, owing to the mastery of natural forces which science has begun to give, there would be more comfort and happiness for all if all devoted themselves to the conquest of Nature rather than of each other. The representation of Nature as a friend, and sometimes as even an ally in our struggles with other men, obscures the true position of man in the world, and diverts his energies from the pursuit of scientific power, which is the only fight that can bring long-continued well-being to the human race.

Apart from all the utilitarian arguments, the search for a happiness based upon untrue beliefs is neither very noble nor very glorious. There is a stark joy in the unflinching perception of our true place in the world, and a more vivid drama than any that is possible to those who hide behind the enclosing walls of myth. There are 'perilous seas' in the world of thought, which can only be sailed by those who are willing to face their own physical powerlessness. And above all, there is liberation from the tyranny of Fear, which blots out the light of day and keeps men grovelling and cruel. No man is liberated from fear who dare not see his place in the world as it is; no man can achieve the greatness of which he is capable until he has allowed himself to see his own littleness.

Chapter 3

Is Science Superstitious?

Modern life is built on science in two respects. On the one hand, we all depend upon scientific inventions and discoveries for our daily bread and for our comforts and amusements. On the other hand, certain habits of mind, connected with a scientific outlook, have spread gradually during the past three centuries from a few men of genius to large sections of the population. These two operations of science are bound up together when we consider sufficiently long periods, but either might exist without the other for several centuries. Until near the end of the eighteenth century the scientific habit of mind did not greatly affect daily life, since it had not led to the great inventions that revolutionised industrial technique. On the other hand, the manner of life produced by science can be taken over by populations which have only certain practical rudiments of scientific knowledge; such populations can make and utilise machines invented elsewhere, and can even make minor improvements in them. If the collective intelligence of mankind were to degenerate, the kind of technique and daily life which science has produced would nevertheless survive, in all probability, for many generations. But it would not survive for ever, because, if seriously disturbed by a cataclysm, it could not be reconstructed.

The scientific outlook, therefore, is a matter of importance to mankind, either for good or evil. But the scientific outlook itself is twofold, like the artistic outlook. The creator and the appreciator are different people and require quite different habits of mind. The scientific creator, like every other, is apt to be inspired by passions to which he gives an intellectualist expression amounting to an undemonstrated faith, without which he would probably achieve little. The appreciator does not need this kind of faith; he can see things in proportion and make necessary reservations, and may regard the creator as a crude and barbaric person in comparison with himself. As civilisation becomes more diffused and more traditional, there is a tendency for the habits of mind of the appeciator to conquer those who might be creators, with the result that the civilisation in question becomes Byzantine and retrospective. Something of this sort seems to be beginning to happen in science. The simple faith which upheld the pioneers is decaying at the centre. Outlying nations, such as the Russians, the Japanese, and the Young Chinese, still welcome science with seventeenth-century fervour; so do the bulk of the populations of Western nations. But the high priests begin to weary of the worship to which they are officially dedicated. The pious young Luther reverenced a free-thinking Pope, who allowed oxen to be sacrificed to Jupiter on the Capitol to promote his recovery from illness. So in our day those remote from centres of culture have a reverence for science which its augurs no longer feel. The 'scientific' materialism of the Bolsheviks, like early German Protestantism, is an attempt to preserve the old piety in a form which both friends and foes believe to be new. But their fiery belief in the verbal inspiration of Newton has only accelerated the spread of scientific scepticism among the 'bourgeois' scientists of the West. Science, as an activity recognised and encouraged by the State, has become politically conservative, except where, as in Tennessee, the State has remained pre-scientific. The fundamental faith of most men of science in the present day is in the importance of preserving the *status quo*. Consequently they are very willing to claim for science no more than its due, and to concede much of the claims of other conservative forces, such as religion.

They are faced, however, with a great difficulty. While the men of science are in the main conservative, science is still the chief agent of rapid change in the world. The emotions produced by the change in Asia, in Africa and among the industrial populations of Europe are often displeasing to those who have a conservative outlook. Hence arises a hesitation as to the value of science which has contributed to the scepticism of the High Priests. If it stood alone, it might be unimportant. But it is reinforced by genuine intellectual difficulties which, if they prove insuperable, are likely to bring the era of scientific discovery to a close. I do not mean that this will happen suddenly. Russia and Asia may continue for another century to entertain the scientific faith which the West is losing. But sooner or later, if the logical case against this faith is irrefutable, it will convince men who, for whatever reason, may be momentarily weary; and, once convinced, they will find it impossible to recapture the old glad confidence. The case against the scientific *credo* deserves, therefore, to be examined with all care.

When I speak of the scientific *credo*, I am not speaking merely of what is logically implied in the view that, in the main, science is true; I am speaking of something more enthusiastic and less rational – namely, the system of beliefs and emotions which lead a man to become a great scientific discoverer. The question is: Can such beliefs and emotions survive among men who have the intellectual powers without which scientific discovery is impossible?

Two very interesting recent books will help us to see the nature of the problem. The books I mean are: Burtt's *Metaphysical Foundations of Modern Science* (1924) and Whitehead's *Science and the Modern World* (1926). Each of these criticises the system of ideas which the modern world owes to Copernicus, Kepler, Galileo, and Newton – the former almost wholly from an historical standpoint, the latter both historically and logically. Dr Whitehead's book is the more important, because it is not merely critical, but constructive, and aims at supplying an intellectually satisfying basis for future science, which is to be at the same time emotionally satisfying to the extra-scientific aspirations of mankind. I cannot accept the logical arguments advanced by Dr Whitehead in favour of what may be called the pleasant parts of his theory: while admitting the need of an intellectual reconstruction of scientific concepts, I incline to the view that the new concepts will be just as disagreeable to our non-intellectual emotions as the old ones, and will therefore be accepted only by those who have a strong emotional bias in favour of science. But let us see what the argument is.

There is, to begin with, the historical aspect. 'There can be no living science,' says Dr Whitehead, 'unless there is a widespread instinctive conviction in the existence of an *order of things*, and, in particular, of an *order of Nature*.' Science could only have been created by men who already had this belief, and therefore the original sources of the belief must have been pre-scientific. Other elements also went to make up the complex mentality required for the rise of science. The Greek view of life, he maintains, was predominantly dramatic, and therefore tended to emphasise the end rather than the beginning: this was a drawback from the point of view of science. On the other hand, Greek tragedy contributed the idea of Fate, which facilitated the view that events are rendered necessary by natural laws. 'Fate in Greek Tragedy becomes the order of Nature in modern thought.' The necessitarian view was reinforced by Roman law. The Roman Government, unlike the Oriental despot, acted (in theory at least) not arbitrarily, but in accordance with rules previously laid down. Similarly, Christianity conceived God as acting in accordance with laws, though they were laws which God Himself had made. All this facilitated the rise of the conception of Natural Law, which is one essential ingredient in scientific mentality.

The non-scientific beliefs which inspired the work of sixteenth- and seventeenth-century pioneers are admirably set forth by Dr Burtt, with the aid of many little-known original sources. It appears, for example, that Kepler's inspiration was, in part, a sort of Zoroastrian sun-worship which he adopted at a critical period of his youth. 'It was primarily by such considerations as the deification of the sun and its proper placing at the centre of the universe that Kepler in the years of his adolescent fervour and warm imagination was induced to accept the new system.' Throughout the Renaissance there is a certain hostility to Christianity, based primarily upon admiration for Pagan antiquity; it did not dare to express itself openly as a rule, but led, for example, to a revival of astrology, which the Church condemned as involving physical determinism. The revolt against Christianity was associated with superstition quite as much as with science – sometimes, as in Kepler's case, with both in intimate union.

But there is another ingredient, equally essential, but absent in the Middle Ages, and not common in antiquity – namely, an interest in 'irreducible and stubborn facts'. Curiosity about facts is found before the Renaissance in individuals – for example, the Emperor Frederick II and Roger Bacon; but at the Renaissance it suddenly becomes common among intelligent people. In Montaigne one finds it without the interest in Natural Law; consequently Montaigne was not a man of science. A peculiar blend of general and particular interests is involved in the pursuit of science; the particular is studied in the hope that it may throw light upon the general. In the Middle Ages it was thought that, theoretically, the particular could be deduced from general principles; in the Renaissance these general principles fell into disrepute, and the passion for historical antiquity produced a strong interest in particular occurrences. This interest, operating upon minds trained by the Greek, Roman and scholastic traditions, produced at last the mental atmosphere which made Kepler and Galileo possible. But naturally something of this atmosphere surrounds their work, and has travelled with it down to their present-day successors. 'Science has never shaken off its origin in the historical revolt of the later Renaissance. It has remained predominantly an anti-rationalistic movement, based upon a naïve faith. What reasoning it has wanted has been borrowed from mathematics, which is a surviving relic of Greek rationalism, following the deductive method. Science repudiates philosophy. In other words, it has never cared to justify its faith or to explain its meaning, and has remained blandly indifferent to its refutation by Hume.'

Can science survive when we separate it from the superstitions which nourished its infancy? The indifference of science to philosophy has been due, of course, to its amazing success; it has increased the sense of human power, and has therefore been on the whole agreeable, in spite of its occasional conflicts with theological orthodoxy. But in quite recent times science has been driven by its own problems to take an interest in philosophy. This is especially true of the theory of relativity, with its merging of space and time into the single space-time order of events. But it is true also of the theory of quanta, with its apparent need of discontinuous motion. Also, in another sphere, physiology and bio-chemistry are making inroads on psychology which threaten philosophy in a vital spot; Dr Watson's Behaviourism is the spear-head of this attack, which, while it involves the opposite of respect for philosophic tradition, nevertheless necessarily rests upon a new philosophy of its own. For such reasons science and philosophy can no longer preserve an armed neutrality, but must be either friends or foes. They cannot be friends unless science can pass the examination which philosophy must set as to its premisses. If they cannot be friends, they can only destroy each other; it is no longer possible that either alone can remain master of the field.

Dr Whitehead offers two things, with a view to the philosophical justification of science. On the one hand, he presents certain new concepts, by means of which the physics of relativity and quanta can be built up in a way which is more satisfying intellectually than any that results from piecemeal amendments to the old conception of solid matter. This part of his work, though not yet developed with the fullness that we may hope to see, lies within science as broadly conceived, and is capable of justification by the usual methods which lead us to prefer one theoretical interpretation of a set of facts to another. It is technically difficult, and I shall say no more about it. From our present point of view, the important aspect of Dr Whitehead's work is its more philosophical portion. He not only offers us a better science, but a philosophy which is to make that science rational, in a sense in which traditional science has not been rational since the time of Hume. This philosophy is, in the main, very similar to that of Bergson. The difficulty which I feel here is that, in so far as Dr Whitehead's new concepts can be embodied in formulae which can be submitted to the ordinary scientific or logical tests, they do not seem to involve his philosophy; his philosophy, therefore, must be accepted on its intrinsic merits. We must not accept it merely on the ground that, if true, it justifies science, for the question at issue is whether science can be justified. We must examine directly whether it seems to us to be true in fact; and here we find ourselves beset with all the old perplexities.

I will take only one point, but it is a crucial one. Bergson, as everyone knows, regards the past as surviving in memory, and also holds that nothing is ever really forgotten; on these points it would seem that Dr Whitehead agrees with him. Now this is all very well as a poetic way of speaking, but it cannot (I should have thought) be accepted as a scientifically accurate way of stating the facts. If I recollect some past event – say my arrival in China – it is a mere figure of speech to say that I am arriving in China over again. Certain words or images occur when I recollect, and are related to what I am recollecting, both causally and by a certain similarity, often little more than a similarity of logical structure. The scientific problem of the relation of a recollection to a past event remains intact, even if we choose to say that the recollection consists of a survival of the past event. For, if we say this, we must nevertheless admit that the event has changed in the interval, and we shall be faced with the scientific problem of finding the laws according to which it changes. Whether we call the recollection a new event or the old event greatly changed can make no difference to the scientific problem.

The great scandals in the philosophy of science ever since the time of Hume have been causality and induction. We all believe in both, but Hume made it appear that our belief is a blind faith for which no rational ground can be assigned. Dr Whitehead believes that his philosophy affords an answer to Hume. So did Kant. I find myself unable to accept either answer. And yet, in common with everyone else, I cannot help believing that there must be an answer. This state of affairs is profoundly unsatisfactory, and becomes more so as science becomes more entangled with philosophy. We must hope that an answer will be found; but I am quite unable to believe that it has been found.

Science as it exists at present is partly agreeable, partly disagreeable. It is agreeable through the power which it gives us of manipulating our environment, and to a small but important minority it is agreeable because it affords intellectual satisfactions. It is disagreeable because, however we may seek to disguise the fact, it assumes a determinism which involves, theoretically, the power of predicting human actions; in this respect it seems to lessen human power. Naturally people wish to keep the pleasant aspect of science without the unpleasant aspect; but so far the attempts to do so have broken down. If we emphasise the fact that our belief in causality and induction is irrational, we must infer that we do not know science to be true, and that it may at any moment cease to give us the control over the environment for the sake of which we like it. This alternative, however, is purely theoretical; it is not one which a modern man can adopt in practice. If, on the other hand, we admit the claims of scientific method, we cannot avoid the conclusion that causality and induction are applicable to human volitions as much as to anything else. All that has happened during the twentieth century in physics, physiology and psychology goes to strengthen this conclusion. The outcome seems to be that, though the rational justification of science is theoretically inadequate, there is no method of securing what is pleasant in science without what is unpleasant. We can do so, of course, by refusing to face the logic of the situation; but, if so, we shall dry up the impulse to scientific discovery at its source, which is the desire to understand the world. It is to be hoped that the future will offer some more satisfactory solution of this tangled problem.

Chapter 4

Can Men Be Rational?

I am in the habit of thinking of myself as a Rationalist; and a Rationalist, I suppose, must be one who wishes men to be rational. But in these days rationality has received many hard knocks, so that it is difficult to know what one means by it, or whether, if that were known, it is something which human beings can achieve. The question of the definition of rationality has two sides, theoretical and practical: what is a rational opinion? and what is rational conduct? Pragmatism emphasises the irrationality of opinion, and psycho-analysis emphasises the irrationality of conduct. Both have led many people to the view that there is no such thing as an ideal of rationality to which opinion and conduct might with advantage conform. It would seem to follow that, if you and I hold different opinions, it is useless to appeal to argument, or to seek the arbitrament of an impartial outsider; there is nothing for us to do but to fight it out, by the methods of rhetoric, advertisement or warfare, according to the degree of our financial and military strength. I believe such an outlook to be very dangerous, and, in the long run, fatal to civilisation. I shall, therefore, endeavour to show that the ideal of rationality remains unaffected by the ideas that have been thought fatal to it, and that it retains all the importance it was formerly believed to have as a guide to thought and life.

To begin with rationality in opinion: I should define it merely as the habit of taking account of all relevant evidence in arriving at a belief. Where certainty is unattainable, a rational man will give most weight to the most probable opinion, while retaining others, which have an appreciable probability, in his mind as hypotheses which subsequent evidence may show to be preferable. This, of course, assumes that it is possible in many cases to ascertain facts and probabilities by an objective method – i.e. a method which will lead any two careful people to the same result. This is often questioned. It is said by many that the only function of intellect is to facilitate the satisfaction of the individual's desires and needs.

The Plebs Text-Books Committee, in their *Outline of Psychology* (p. 68), say: '*The intellect is above all things an instrument of partiality.* Its function is to secure that those actions which are beneficial to the individual or the species shall be performed, and that those actions which are less beneficial shall be inhibited.' (Italics in the original.)

But the same authors, in the same book (p. 123), state, again in italics: '*The faith of the Marxian differs profoundly from religious faith; the latter is based only on desire and tradition; the former is grounded on the scientific analysis of objective reality.*' This seems inconsistent with what they say about the intellect, unless, indeed, they mean to suggest that it is not intellect which has led them to adopt the Marxian faith. In any case, since they admit that 'scientific analysis of objective reality' is possible, they must admit that it is possible to have opinions which are rational in an objective sense.

More erudite authors who advocate an irrationalist point of view, such as the pragmatist philosophers, are not to be caught out so easily. They maintain that there is no such thing as objective fact to which our opinions must conform if they are to be true. For them opinions are merely weapons in the struggle for existence, and those which help a man to survive are to be called 'true'. This view was prevalent in Japan in the sixth century AD, when Buddhism first reached that country. The Government, being in doubt as to the truth of the new religion, ordered one of the courtiers to adopt it experimentally; if he prospered more than the others, the religion was to be adopted universally. This is the method (with modifications to suit modern times) which the pragmatists advocate in regard to all religious controversies; and yet I have not heard of any who have announced their conversion to the Jewish faith, although it seems to lead to prosperity more rapidly than any other.

In spite of the pragmatist's definition of 'truth', however, he has always, in ordinary life, a quite different standard for the less refined questions which arise in practical affairs. A pragmatist on a jury in a murder case will weigh the evidence exactly as any other man will, whereas if he adopted his professed criterion he ought to consider whom among the population it would be most profitable to hang. That man would be, by definition, guilty of the murder, since belief in his guilt would be more useful, and therefore more 'true', than belief in the guilt of anyone else. I am afraid such practical pragmatism does sometimes occur; I have heard of 'frame-ups' in America and Russia which answered this description. But in such cases all possible efforts after concealment are made, and if they fail there is a scandal. This effort after concealment shows that even policemen believe in objective truth in the case of a criminal trial. It is this kind of objective truth – a very mundane and pedestrian affair – that is sought in science. It is this kind also that is sought in religion so long as people hope to find it. It is only when people have given up the hope of proving that religion is true in a straightforward sense that they set to work to prove that it is 'true' in some new-fangled sense. It may be laid down broadly that irrationalism, i.e. disbelief in objective fact, arises almost always from the desire to assert something for which there is no evidence, or to deny something for which there is very good evidence. But the belief in objective fact always persists as regards particular practical questions, such as investments or engaging servants. And if fact can be made the test of the truth of our beliefs anywhere, it should be the test everywhere, leading to agnosticism wherever it cannot be applied.

The above considerations are, of course, very inadequate to their theme. The question of the objectivity of fact has been rendered difficult by the obfuscations of philosophers, with which I have attempted to deal elsewhere in a more thoroughgoing fashion. For the present I shall assume that there are facts, that some facts can be known, and that in regard to certain others a degree of probability can be ascertained in relation to facts which can be known. Our beliefs are, however, often contrary to fact; even when we only hold that something is probable on the evidence, it may be that we ought to hold it to be improbable on the same evidence. The theoretical part of rationality, then, will consist in basing our beliefs as regards matters of fact upon evidence rather than upon wishes, prejudices, or traditions. According to the subject-matter, a rational man will be the same as one who is judicial or one who is scientific.

There are some who think that psycho-analysis has shown the impossibility of being rational in our beliefs, by pointing out the strange and almost lunatic origin of many people's cherished convictions. I have a very high respect for psycho-analysis, and I believe that it can be enormously useful. But the popular mind has somewhat lost sight of the purpose which has mainly inspired Freud and his followers. Their method is primarily one of therapeutics, a way of curing hysteria and various kinds of insanity. During the war psycho-analysis proved to be far the most potent treatment for war-neuroses. Rivers's *Instinct and the Unconscious*, which is largely based upon experience of 'shell-shock' patients, gives a beautiful analysis of the morbid effects of fear when it cannot be straightforwardly indulged. These effects, of course, are largely non-intellectual; they include various kinds of paralysis, and all sorts of apparently physical ailments. With these, for the moment, we are not concerned; it is intellectual derangements that form our theme. It is found that many of the delusions of lunatics result from instinctive obstructions, and can be cured by purely mental means – i.e. by making the patient bring to mind facts of which he had repressed the memory. This kind of treatment, and the outlook which inspires it, pre-suppose an ideal of sanity, from which the patient has departed, and to which he is to be brought back by making him conscious of all the relevant facts, including those which he most wishes to forget. This is the exact opposite of that lazy acquiescence in irrationality which is sometimes urged by those who only know that psycho-analysis has shown the prevalence of irrational beliefs, and who forget or ignore that its purpose is to diminish this prevalence by a definite method of medical treatment. A closely similar method can cure the irrationalities of those who are not recognised lunatics, provided they will submit to treatment by a practitioner free from their delusions. Presidents, Cabinet Ministers and Eminent Persons, however, seldom fulfil this condition, and therefore remain uncured.

So far, we have been considering only the theoretical side of rationality. The practical side, to which we must now turn our attention, is more difficult. Differences of opinion on practical questions spring from two sources: first, differences between the desires of the disputants; secondly, differences in their estimates of the means for realising their desires. Differences of the second kind are really theoretical, and only derivatively practical. For example, some authorities hold that our first line of defence should consist of battleships, others that it should consist of aeroplanes. Here there is no difference as regards the end proposed, namely, national defence, but only as to the means. The argument can therefore be conducted in a purely scientific manner, since the disagreement which causes the dispute is only as to facts, present or future, certain or probable. To all such cases the kind of rationality which I called theoretical applies, in spite of the fact that a practical issue is involved.

There is, however, in many cases which appear to come under this head a complication which is very important in practice. A man who desires to act in a certain way will persuade himself that by so acting he will achieve some end which he considers good, even when, if he had no such desire, he would see no reason for such a belief. And he will judge quite differently as to matters of fact and as to probabilities from the way in which a man with contrary desires will judge. Gamblers, as everyone knows, are full of irrational beliefs as to systems which *must* lead them to win in the long run. People who take an interest in politics persuade themselves that the leaders of their party would never be guilty of the knavish tricks practised by opposing politicians. Men who like administration think that it is good for the populace to be treated like a herd of sheep, men who like tobacco say that it soothes the nerves, and men who like alcohol say that it stimulates wit. The bias produced by such causes falsifies men's judgements as to facts in a way which is very hard to avoid. Even a learned scientific article about the effects of alcohol on the nervous system will generally betray by internal evidence whether the author is or is not a teetotaller; in either case he has a tendency to see the facts in the way that would justify his own practice. In politics and religion such considerations become very important. Most men think that in framing their political opinions they are actuated by desire for the public good; but nine times out of ten a man's politics can be predicted from the way in which he makes his living. This has led some people to maintain, and many more to believe practically, that in such matters it is impossible to be objective, and that no method is possible except a tug-of-war between classes with opposite bias.

It is just in such matters, however, that psycho-analysis is particularly useful, since it enables man to become aware of a bias which has hitherto been unconscious. It gives a technique for seeing ourselves as others see us, and a reason for supposing that this view of ourselves is less unjust than we are inclined to think. Combined with a training in the scientific outlook, this method could, if it were widely taught, enable people to be infinitely more rational than they are at present as regards all their beliefs about matters of fact, and about the probable effect of any proposed action. And if men did not disagree about such matters, the disagreements which might survive would almost certainly be found capable of amicable adjustment.

There remains, however, a residuum which cannot be treated by purely intellectual methods. The desires of one man do not by any means harmonise completely with those of another. Two competitors on the Stock Exchange might be in complete agreement as to what would be the effect of this or that action, but this would not produce practical harmony, since each wishes to grow rich at the expense of the other. Yet even here rationality is capable of preventing most of the harm that might otherwise occur. We call a man irrational when he acts in a passion, when he cuts off his nose to spite his face. He is irrational because he forgets that, by indulging the desire which he happens to feel most strongly at the moment, he will thwart other desires which in the long run are more important to him. If men were rational, they would take a more correct view of their own interest than they do at present; and if all men acted from enlightened self-interest the world would be a paradise in comparison with what it is. I do not maintain that there is nothing better than self-interest as a motive to action; but I do maintain that self-interest, like altruism, is better when it is enlightened than when it is unenlightened. In an ordered community it is very rarely to a man's interest to do anything which is very harmful to others. The less rational a man is, the oftener he will fail to perceive how what injures others also injures him, because hatred or envy will blind him. Therefore, although I do not pretend that enlightened self-interest is the highest morality, I do maintain that, if it became common, it would make the world an immeasurably better place than it is.

Rationality in practice may be defined as the habit of remembering all our relevant desires, and not only the one which happens at the moment to be strongest. Like rationality in opinion, it is a matter of degree. Complete rationality is no doubt an unattainable ideal, but so long as we continue to classify some men as lunatics it is clear that we think some men more rational than others. I believe that all solid progress in the world consists of an increase in rationality, both practical and theoretical. To preach an altruistic

morality appears to me somewhat useless, because it will appeal
only to those who already have altruistic desires. But to preach
rationality is somewhat different, since rationality helps us to realise our own desires on the whole, whatever they may be. A man
is rational in proportion as his intelligence informs and controls
his desires. I believe that the control of our acts by our intelligence
is ultimately what is of most importance, and what alone will
make social life remain possible as science increases the means at
our disposal for injuring each other. Education, the press, politics,
religion – in a word, all the great forces in the world – are at
present on the side of irrationality; they are in the hands of men
who flatter King Demos in order to lead him astray. The remedy
does not lie in anything heroically cataclysmic, but in the efforts of
individuals towards a more sane and balanced view of our relations to our neighbours and to the world. It is to intelligence,
increasingly wide-spread, that we must look for the solution of the
ills from which our world is suffering.

Chapter 5

Philosophy in the Twentieth Century

Ever since the end of the Middle Ages philosophy has steadily declined in social and political importance. William of Ockham, one of the greatest of mediaeval philosophers, was hired by the Kaiser to write pamphlets against the Pope; in those days many burning questions were bound up with disputes in the schools. The advances of philosophy in the seventeenth century were more or less connected with political opposition to the Catholic Church; Malebranche, it is true, was a priest, but priests are not now allowed to accept his philosophy. The disciples of Locke in eighteenth-century France, and the Benthamites in nineteenth-century England, were for the most part extreme Radicals in politics, and created the modern bourgeois liberal outlook. But the correlation between philosophical and political opinions grows less definite as we advance. Hume was a Tory in politics, though an extreme Radical in philosophy. Only in Russia, which remained mediaeval till the Revolution, has any clear connection of philosophy and politics survived. Bolsheviks are materialists, while Whites are idealists. In Tibet the connection is even closer; the second official in the State is called the 'metaphysician in chief'. Elsewhere philosophy is no longer held in such high esteem.

Academic philosophy, throughout the twentieth century, has been mainly divided into three groups. The first consists of the adherents of the classical German philosophy, usually Kant, but sometimes Hegel. The second consists of the pragmatists and Bergson. The third consists of those who attach themselves to the sciences, believing that philosophy has no special brand of truth and no peculiar method of arriving at it; these men, for convenience, may be called realists, though in fact there are many among them to whom this name is not strictly applicable. The distinction between the different schools is not sharp, and individuals belong partly to one, partly to another. William James may be regarded as almost the founder of both realism and pragmatism. Dr Whitehead's recent books employ the methods of realists in defence of a more or less Bergsonian metaphysic. Many philosophers, not without a considerable show of reason, regard Einstein's doctrines as affording a scientific basis for Kant's belief in the subjectivity of time and space. The distinctions in fact are thus less clear than the distinctions in logic. Nevertheless the distinctions in logic are useful as affording a framework for the classification of opinions.

German idealism, throughout the twentieth century, has been on the defensive. The new books that have been recognised as important by others than professors have represented newer schools, and a person who judged by book reviews might imagine that these schools had now the upper hand. But in fact most teachers of philosophy, in Germany, France and Great Britain, though perhaps not America, still adhere to the classical tradition. It is certainly much easier for a young man to get a post if he belongs to this party than if he does not. Its opponents made an attempt to show that it shared the wickedness of everything German, and was in some way responsible for the invasion of Belgium.[1] But its adherents were too eminent and respectable for this line of attack to be successful. Two of them, Émile Boutroux and Bernard Bosanquet, were until their deaths the official spokesmen of French and British philosophy respectively at international congresses. Religion and conservatism look mainly to this school for defence against heresy and revolution. They have the strength and weakness of those who stand for the *status quo*: the strength that comes of tradition, and the weakness that comes of lack of fresh thought.

In the English-speaking world, this position was only acquired just before the beginning of the twentieth century. I began the serious study of philosophy in the year 1893, the year which saw the publication of Mr Bradley's *Appearance and Reality*. Mr Bradley was one of those who had had to fight to win proper recognition of German philosophy in England, and his attitude was very far from that of one who defends a traditional orthodoxy. To me, as to most of my contemporaries, his *Logic* and his

[1] See e.g. Santayana's *Egotism in German Philosophy*.

Appearance and Reality made a profound appeal. I still regard these books with the greatest respect, though I have long ceased to agree with their doctrines.

The outlook of Hegelianism is characterised by the belief that logic alone can tell us a great deal about the real world. Mr Bradley shares this belief; he contends that the world as it seems to be is self-contradictory, and therefore illusory, while the real world, since it must be logically self-consistent, is bound to have certain characteristics of a surprising kind. It cannot be in time and space, it cannot contain a variety of interrelated things, it cannot contain separate selves, or even that degree of division between subject and object which is involved in knowing. It consists therefore of a single Absolute, timelessly engaged in something more analogous to feeling than to thinking or willing. Our sublunary world is all illusion, and what seems to happen in it does not really matter. This doctrine ought to destroy morality, but morality is temperamental and defies logic. Hegelians in fact urge as their basic moral principle that we ought to behave as if the Hegelian philosophy were true; but they do not notice that if it were true it would not matter how we behave.

The attack upon this philosophy came from two sides. On the one side were the logicians, who pointed to fallacies in Hegel, and contended that relations and plurality, space and time, are in fact not self-contradictory. On the other side were those who disliked the regimentation and orderliness involved in a world created by logic; of these the chief were William James and Bergson. The two lines of attack were not logically inconsistent, except in some of their accidental manifestations, but they were temperamentally different, and were inspired by different kinds of knowledge. Moreover their appeal was quite different; the appeal of the one was academic, that of the other was human. The academic appeal argued that Hegelianism was false: the human appeal argued that it was disagreeable. Naturally the latter had more popular success.

In the English-speaking world, the greatest influence in the overthrow of German idealism was William James – not as he appears in his *Psychology*, but as he came to be known through the series of small books which were published in the last years of his life and after his death. In an article published in *Mind* so long ago as 1884, reprinted in the posthumous volume *Essays in*

Radical Empiricism,[1] he sets out his temperamental bias with extraordinary charm:

'Since we are in the main not sceptics, we might go on and frankly confess to each other the motives for our several faiths. I frankly confess mine – I cannot but think that at bottom they are of an aesthetic and not of a logical sort. The 'through-and-through' universe seems to suffocate me with its infallible impeccable all-pervasiveness. Its necessity, with no possibilities; its relations, with no subjects, make me feel as if I had entered into a contract with no reserved rights, or rather as if I had to live in a large seaside boarding-house with no private bedroom in which I might take refuge from the society of the place. I am distinctly aware, moreover, that the old quarrel of sinner and pharisee has something to do with the matter. Certainly, to my personal knowledge, all Hegelians are not prigs, but I somehow feel as if all prigs ought to end, if developed, by becoming Hegelians. There is a story of two clergymen asked by mistake to conduct the same funeral. One came first and had got no further than "I am the Resurrection and the Life" when the other entered. "*I* am the Resurrection and the Life," cried the latter. The "through-and-through" philosophy, as it actually exists, reminds many of us of that clergyman. It seems too buttoned-up and white-chokered and clean-shaven a thing to speak for the vast slow-breathing unconscious Kosmos with its dread abysses and its unknown tides.'

I think it may be wagered that no one except William James has ever lived who would have thought of comparing Hegelianism to a seaside boarding-house. In 1884 this article had no effect, because Hegelianism was still on the up-grade, and philosophers had not learnt to admit that their temperaments had anything to do with their opinions. In 1912 (the date of the reprint) the atmosphere had changed through many causes – among others the influence of William James upon his pupils. I cannot claim to have known him more than superficially except from his writings, but it seems to me that one may distinguish three strands in his nature, all of which contributed to form his outlook. Last in time but first in its philosophical manifestations was the influence of his training in

[1] Pp. 276–8.

physiology and medicine, which gave him a scientific and slightly materialistic bias as compared to purely literary philosophers who derived their inspiration from Plato, Aristotle and Hegel. This strand dominates his *Psychology* except in a few crucial passages, such as his discussion of free will. The second element in his philosophical make-up was a mystical and religious bias inherited from his father and shared with his brother. This inspired the *Will to Believe* and his interest in psychical research. Thirdly, there was an attempt, made with all the earnestness of a New England conscience, to exterminate the natural fastidiousness which he also shared with his brother, and replace it by democratic sentiment à la Walt Whitman. The fastidiousness is visible in the above quotation, where he expresses horror of a boarding-house with no private bedroom (which Whitman would have loved). The wish to be democratic is visible in the claim that he is a sinner, not a pharisee. Certainly he was not a pharisee, but he probably committed as few sins as any man who ever lived. On this point he fell short of his usual modesty.

The best people usually owe their excellence to a combination of qualities which might have been supposed incompatible, and so it was in the case of James, whose importance was greater than was thought by most of his contemporaries. He advocated pragmatism as a method of presenting religious hopes as scientific hypotheses, and he adopted the revolutionary view that there is no such thing as 'consciousness', as a way of overcoming the opposition between mind and matter without giving predominance to either. In these two parts of his philosophy he had different allies: Schiller and Bergson as regards the former, the new realists as regards the latter. Only Dewey, among eminent men, was with him on both issues. The two parts have different histories and affiliations, and must be considered separately.

James's *Will to Believe* dates from 1897; his *Pragmatism* from 1907. Schiller's *Humanism* and Dewey's *Studies in Logical Theory* both date from 1903. Throughout the early years of the twentieth century the philosophical world was excited about pragmatism; then Bergson outbid it in appealing to the same tastes. The three founders of pragmatism differ greatly *inter se*; we may distinguish James, Schiller and Dewey as respectively its religious, literary and scientific protagonists – for, though James was many-sided, it was chiefly his religious side which found an outlet in pragmatism. But let us ignore these differences and try to present the doctrine as a unity.

The basis of the doctrine is a certain kind of scepticism. Traditional philosophy professed to be able to prove the fundamental doctrines of religion; its opponents professed to be able to disprove them, or at least, like Spencer, to prove that they could not be proved. It seemed, however, that if they could not be proved, they also could not be disproved. And this appeared to be the case with many doctrines which such men as Spencer regarded as unshakable: causality, the reign of law, the general trustworthiness of memory, the validity of induction, and so on. All these, from a purely rational point of view, should be embraced in the agnostic's suspense of judgement, since, so far as we can see, they are radically incapable of proof or disproof. James argued that, as practical men, we cannot remain in doubt on these issues if we are to survive. We must assume, for instance, that the sort of food which has nourished us in the past will not poison us in the future. Sometimes we are mistaken, and die. The test of a belief is not conformity with 'fact', since we can never reach the facts concerned; the test is its success in promoting life and the achievement of our desires. From this point of view, as James tried to show in *The Varieties of Religious Experience*, religious beliefs often pass the test, and are therefore to be called 'true'. It is in no other sense – so he contends – that the most accredited theories of science can be called 'true': they work in practice, and that is all we know about it.

As applied to the general hypotheses of science and religion, there is a great deal to be said for this view. Given a careful definition of what is meant by 'working', and a proviso that the cases concerned are those where we do not really know the truth, there is no need to quarrel with the doctrine in this region. But let us take humbler examples, where real truth is not so hard to obtain. Suppose you see a flash of lightning, you may expect to hear thunder, or you may judge that the flash was too distant for the thunder to be audible, or you may not think about the matter at all. This last is usually the most sensible course, but let us suppose that you adopt one of the other two. When you hear the thunder, your belief is verified or refuted, not by any advantage or disadvantage it has brought you, but by a 'fact', the sensation of hearing thunder. Pragmatists attend mainly to beliefs which are incapable of being verified by any facts that come within our experience. Most of our everyday beliefs about mundane affairs – e.g. that so-and-so's address is such-and-such – are capable of verification within our experience, and in these cases the pragmatist's criterion is unnecessary. In many cases, like the above instance of the thunder, it is quite inapplicable, since the true belief has no practical advantage over the false one, and neither is as advantageous as thinking about something else. It is a common defect of philosophers to like 'grand' examples rather than such as come from ordinary daily life.

Although pragmatism may not contain ultimate philosophical truth, it has certain important merits. First, it realises that the truth that *we* can attain to is merely human truth, fallible and changeable like everything human. What lies outside the cycle of human occurrences is not truth, but fact (of certain kinds). Truth is a property of beliefs, and beliefs are psychical events. Moreover their relation to facts does not have the schematic simplicity which logic assumes; to have pointed this out is a second merit in pragmatism. Beliefs are vague and complex, pointing not to one precise fact, but to several vague regions of fact. Beliefs, therefore, unlike the schematic propositions of logic, are not sharply opposed as true or false, but are a blur of truth and falsehood; they are of varying shades of grey, never white or black. People who speak with reverence of the 'Truth' would do better to speak about Fact, and to realise that the reverend qualities to which they pay homage are not to be found in human beliefs. There are practical as well as theoretical advantages in this, since people persecute each other because they believe that they know the 'Truth'. Speaking psycho-analytically, it may be laid down that any 'great ideal' which people mention with awe is really an excuse for inflicting pain on their enemies. Good wine needs no bush, and good morals need no bated breath.

In practice, however, pragmatism has a more sinister side. The truth, it says, is what pays in the way of beliefs. Now a belief may be made to pay through the operation of the criminal law. In the seventeenth century, Catholicism paid in Catholic countries and Protestantism in Protestant countries. Energetic people can manufacture 'truth' by getting hold of the Government and persecuting opinions other than their own. These consequences flow from an exaggeration into which pragmatism has fallen. Granted that, as pragmatists point out, truth is a matter of degree, and is a property of purely human occurrences, namely beliefs, it still does not follow that the degree of truth possessed by a belief depends upon purely human conditions. In increasing the degree of truth in our beliefs, we are approximating to an ideal, and the ideal is determined by Fact, which is only within our control to a certain very limited extent, as regards some of the minor circumstances on or near the surface of a certain planet. The theory of the pragmatist is derived from the practice of the advertiser, who, by saying repeatedly that his pills are worth a guinea a box, makes people willing to give sixpence a box for them, and thus makes his assertion more nearly true than if it had been made with less confidence. Such instances of man-made truth are interesting, but their scope is very limited. By exaggerating their scope, people become involved in an orgy of propaganda, which is ultimately brought to an abrupt end by hard facts in the shape of war, pestilence and famine. The recent history of Europe is an object-lesson of the falsehood of pragmatism in this form.

It is a curious thing that Bergson should have been hailed as an ally by the pragmatists, since, on the face of it, his philosophy is the exact antithesis to theirs. While pragmatists teach that utility is the test of truth, Bergson teaches, on the contrary, that our intellect, having been fashioned by practical needs, ignores all the aspects of the world which it does not pay to notice, and is in fact an obstacle to the apprehension of truth. We have, he thinks, a faculty called 'intuition' which we can use if we take the trouble, and which will enable us to know, in theory at least, everything past and present, though apparently not the future. But since it would be inconvenient to be troubled with so much knowledge, we have developed a brain, the function of which is to forget. But for the brain, we should remember everything; owing to its sieve-like operations, we usually remember only what is useful, and that all wrong. Utility, for Bergson, is the source of error, while truth is arrived at by a mystic contemplation from which all thought of practical advantage is absent. Nevertheless Bergson, like the pragmatists, prefers action to reason, Othello to Hamlet; he thinks it better to kill Desdemona by intuition than to let the King live because of intellect. It is this that makes pragmatists regard him as an ally.

Bergson's *Donnés Immédiates de la Conscience* was published in 1889, and his *Matière et Mémoire* in 1896. But his great reputation began with *L'Evolution Créatrice*, published in 1907 – not that this book was better than the others, but that it contained less argument and more rhetoric, so that it had more persuasive effect. This book contains, from beginning to end, no argument, and therefore no bad argument; it contains merely a poetical picture appealing to the fancy. There is nothing in it to help us to a conclusion as to whether the philosophy which it advocates is true or false; this question, which might be thought not unimportant, Bergson has left to others. But according to his own theories he is right in this, since truth is to be attained by intuition, not by intellect, and is therefore not a matter of argument.

A great part of Bergson's philosophy is merely traditional mysticism expressed in slightly novel language. The doctrine of interpenetration, according to which different things are not really separate, but are merely so conceived by the analytic intellect, is to be found in every mystic, eastern or western, from Parmenides to Mr Bradley. Bergson has given an air of novelty to this doctrine by means of two devices. First, he connects 'intuition' with the instincts of animals; he suggests that intuition is what enables the solitary wasp Ammophila to sting the larva in which it lays its eggs exactly so as to paralyse it without killing it. (The instance is unfortunate, since Dr and Mrs Peckham have shown that this poor wasp is no more unerring than a mere man of science with his blundering intellect.) This gives a flavour of modern science to his doctrines, and enables him to adduce zoological instances which make the unwary think that his views are based upon the latest results of biological research. Secondly, he gives the name 'space' to the separateness of things as they appear to the analytic intellect, and the name 'time' or 'duration' to their interpenetration as revealed to intuition. This enables him to say many new things about 'space' and 'time', which sound very profound and original when they are supposed to be about what is ordinarily meant by those words. 'Matter', being that which is in 'space', is of course a fiction created by the intellect, and is seen to be such as soon as we place ourselves at the point of view of intuition.

In this part of his philosophy, apart from phraseology, Bergson has added nothing to Plotinus. The invention of the phraseology certainly shows great ability, but it is that of the company-pro-moter rather than the philosopher. It is not this part of his phil-osophy, however, which has won him his wide popularity. He owes that to his doctrine of the *élan vital* and real becoming. His great and remarkable innovation is to have combined mysticism with a belief in the reality of time and progress. It is worth while to see how he achieved this feat.

Traditional mysticism has been contemplative, convinced of the unreality of time, and essentially a lazy man's philosophy. The psychological prelude to the mystic illumination is the 'dark night of the soul', which arises when a man is hopelessly balked in his practical activities, or for some reason suddenly loses interest in them. Activity being thus ruled out, he takes to contemplation. It is law of our being that, whenever it is in any way possible, we adopt such beliefs as will preserve our self-respect. Psycho-an-alytic literature is full of grotesque examples of this law. Accord-ingly the man who has been driven to contemplation presently discovers that contemplation is the true end of life, and that the real world is hidden from those who are immersed in mundane activities. From this basis the remaining doctrines of traditional mysticism can be deduced. Lao-Tze, perhaps the first of the great mystics, wrote his book (so tradition avers) at a custom-house while he was waiting to have his baggage examined;[1] and, as might be expected, it is full of the doctrine that action is futile.

But Bergson sought to adapt mysticism to those who believe in activity and 'life', who believe in the reality of progress and are in no way disillusioned about our existence here below. The mystic is usually a temperamentally active man forced into inaction; the vitalist is a temperamentally inactive man with a romantic admir-ation for action. Before 1914 the world was full of such people, 'Heartbreak House' people. Their temperamental basis is bore-dom and scepticism, leading to love of excitement and longing for an irrational faith — a faith which they found ultimately in the belief that it was their duty to make other people kill each other. But in 1907 they had not this outlet, and Bergson provided a good substitute.

Bergson's view is sometimes expressed in language which might mislead, because things which he regards as illusory are occasion-

[1] The chief argument against this tradition is that the book is not very long.

ally mentioned in a way which suggests that they are real. But when we avoid these possibilities of misunderstanding, I think his doctrine of time is as follows. Time is not a series of separate moments or events, but a continuous growth, in which the future cannot be foreseen because it is genuinely new and therefore unimaginable. Everything that really happens persists, like the successive rings in the growth of a tree. (This is not his illustration.) Thus the world is perpetually growing fuller and richer. Everything that has happened persists in the pure memory of intuition, as opposed to the pseudo-memory of the brain. This persistence is 'duration', while the impulse to new creation is the 'élan vital'. To recover the pure memory of intuition is a matter of self-discipline. We are not told how to do it, but one suspects something not unlike the practices of Yogis.

If one might venture to apply to Bergson's philosophy so vulgar a thing as logic, certain difficulties would appear in this philosophy of change. Bergson is never tired of pouring scorn upon the mathematician for regarding time as a series, whose parts are mutually external. But if there is indeed genuine novelty in the world, as he insists (and without this feature his philosophy loses its attractive qualities), and if whatever really comes into the world persists (which is the simple essence of his doctrine of duration), then the sum-total of existence at any earlier time is part of the sum-total at any later time. Total states of the world at various times form a series in virtue of this relation of whole and part, and this series has all the properties that the mathematician wants and that Bergson professes to have banished. If the new elements which are added in later states of the world are not external to the old elements, there is no genuine novelty, creative evolution has created nothing, and we are back in the system of Plotinus. Of course Bergson's answer to this dilemma is that what happens is 'growth', in which everything changes and yet remains the same. This conception, however, is a mystery, which the profane cannot hope to fathom. At bottom, Bergson's appeal is to mystical faith, not to reason; but into the regions where faith is above logic we cannot follow him.

Meanwhile, from many directions, a philosophy grew up which is often described as 'realism', but is really characterised by analysis as a method and pluralism as a metaphysic. It is not necessarily realistic, since it is, in some forms, compatible with

Berkleian idealism. It is not compatible with Kantian or Hegelian idealism, because it rejects the logic upon which those systems are based. It tends more and more to the adoption and development of James's view, that the fundamental stuff of the world is neither mental nor material, but something simpler and more fundamental, out of which both mind and matter are constructed.

In the nineties, James was almost the only eminent figure, except among the very old, that stood out against German idealism. Schiller and Dewey had not yet begun to make themselves felt, and even James was regarded as a psychologist who need not be taken very seriously in philosophy. But with the year 1900 a revolt against German idealism began, not from a pragmatist point of view, but from a severely technical standpoint. In Germany, apart from the admirable works of Frege (which begin in 1879, but were not read until recent years), Husserl's *Logische Untersuchungen*, a monumental work published in 1900, soon began to exert a great effect. Meinong's *Ueber Annahmen* (1902) and *Gegenstandstheorie und Psychologie* (1904) were influential in the same direction. In England, G. E. Moore and I began to advocate similar views. His article on *The Nature of Judgment* was published in 1899; his *Principia Ethica* in 1903. My *Philosophy of Leibniz* appeared in 1900, and *Principles of Mathematics* in 1903. In France, the same kind of philosophy was vigorously championed by Couturat. In America, William James's radical empiricism (without his pragmatism) was blended with the new logic to produce a radically new philosophy, that of the *New Realists*, somewhat later in date, but more revolutionary, than the European works mentioned above, although Mach's *Analyse der Empfindungen* had anticipated part of its teaching.

The new philosophy which was thus inaugurated has not yet reached a final form, and is still in some respects immature. Moreover, there is a very considerable measure of disagreement among its various advocates. It is in parts somewhat abstruse. For these reasons, it is impossible to do more than set forth some of its salient features.

The first characteristic of the new philosophy is that it abandons the claim to a special philosophic method or a peculiar brand of knowledge to be obtained by its means. It regards philosophy as essentially one with science, differing from the special sciences merely by the generality of its problems, and by the fact that it is concerned with the formation of hypotheses where empirical evidence is still lacking. It conceives that all knowledge is scientific knowledge, to be ascertained and proved by the methods of science. It does not aim, as previous philosophy has usually done, at statements about the universe as a whole, nor at the construction of a comprehensive system. It believes, on the basis of its logic, that there is no reason to deny the apparently piecemeal and higgledy-piggledy nature of the world. It does not regard the world as 'organic', in the sense that, from any part adequately understood, the whole could be inferred as the skeleton of an extinct monster can be inferred from a single bone. In particular, it does not attempt, as German idealism did, to deduce the nature of the world as a whole from the nature of knowledge. It regards knowledge as a natural fact like another, with no mystic significance and no cosmic importance.

The new philosophy had originally three main sources: theory of knowledge, logic, and the principles of mathematics. Ever since Kant, knowledge had been conceived as an interaction, in which the thing known was modified by our knowledge of it, and therefore always had certain characteristics due to our knowledge. It was also held (though not by Kant) to be logically impossible for a thing to exist without being known. Therefore the properties acquired through being known were properties which everything must have. In this way, it was contended, we can discover a great deal about the real world by merely studying the conditions of knowledge. The new philosophy maintained, on the contrary, that knowledge, as a rule, makes no difference to what is known, and that there is not the slightest reason why there should not be things which are not known to any mind. Consequently theory of knowledge ceases to be a magic key to open the door to the mysteries of the universe, and we are thrown back upon the plodding investigations of science.

In logic, similarly, atomism replaced the 'organic' view. It had been maintained that everything is affected in its intrinsic nature by its relations to everything else, so that a thorough knowledge of one thing would involve a thorough knowledge of the whole universe. The new logic maintained that the intrinsic character of a thing does not logically enable us to deduce its relations to other things. An example will make the point clear. Leibniz maintains somewhere (and in this he agrees with modern idealists) that if a man is in Europe and his wife dies in India, there is an intrinsic change in the man at the moment of his wife's death. Common sense would say that there is no intrinsic change in the man until he hears of his bereavement. This view is adopted by the new philosophy; its consequences are more far-reaching than they might appear to be at first sight.

The principles of mathematics have always had an important relation to philosophy. Mathematics apparently contains *a priori* knowledge of a high degree of certainty, and most philosophy aspires to *a priori* knowledge. Ever since Zeno the Eleatic, philosophers of an idealistic cast have sought to throw discredit on mathematics by manufacturing contradictions which were designed to show that mathematicians had not arrived at real metaphysical truth, and that the philosophers were able to supply a better brand. There is a great deal of this in Kant, and still more in Hegel. During the nineteenth century, the mathematicians destroyed this part of Kant's philosophy. Lobatchevski, by inventing non-Euclidean geometry, undermined the mathematical argument of Kant's transcendental aesthetic. Weierstrass proved that continuity does not involve infinitesimals; Georg Cantor invented a theory of continuity and a theory of infinity which did away with all the old paradoxes upon which philosophers had battened. Frege showed that arithmetic follows from logic, which Kant had denied. All these results were obtained by ordinary mathematical methods, and were as indubitable as the multiplication table. Philosophers met the situation by not reading the authors concerned. Only the new philosophy assimilated the new results, and thereby won an easy argumentative victory over the partisans of continued ignorance.

The new philosophy is not merely critical. It is constructive, but as science is constructive, bit by bit and tentatively. It has a special technical method of construction, namely, mathematical logic, a new branch of mathematics, much more akin to philosophy than any of the traditional branches. Mathematical logic makes it possible, as it never was before, to see what is the outcome, for philosophy, of a given body of scientific doctrine, what entities must be assumed, and what relations between them. The philosophy of mathematics and physics has made immense advances by the help of this method; part of the outcome for physics has been set forth by Dr Whitehead in three recent works.[1] There is reason to hope that the method will prove equally fruitful in other fields, but it is too technical to be set forth here.

A good deal of modern pluralist philosophy has been inspired by the logical analysis of propositions. At first this method was applied with too much respect for grammar; Meinong, for example, maintained that, since we can say truly 'the round square does not exist', there must be such an object as the round square, although it must be a non-existent object. The present writer was at first not exempt from this kind of reasoning, but discovered in 1905 how to escape from it by means of the theory of 'descriptions', from which it appears that the round square is not mentioned when we say 'the round square does not exist'. It may seem absurd to spend time on such a ridiculous topic as the round square, but such topics often afford the best tests of logical theories. Most logical theories are condemned by the fact that they lead to absurdities; therefore the logician must be aware of absurdities and on the lookout for them. Many laboratory experiments would seem trivial to anyone who did not know their relevance, and absurdities are the experiments of the logician.

From preoccupation with the logical analysis of propositions, the new philosophy had at first a strong tincture of Platonic and mediaeval realism; it regarded abstracts as having the same kind of existence that concretes have. From this view, as its logic perfected itself, it became gradually more free. What remains is not such as to shock common sense.

Although pure mathematics was more concerned than any other science in the first beginnings of the new philosophy, the most important influence in the present day is physics. This has come about chiefly through the work of Einstein, which has fundamentally altered our notions of space, time and matter. This is not the place for an explanation of the theory of relativity, but a few words on some of its philosophical consequences are unavoidable.

Two specially important items in the theory of relativity, from the philosophical point of view, are: (1) that there is not a single all-embracing time in which all the events in the universe have

[1] *The Principles of Natural Knowledge*, 1919; *The Concept of Nature*, 1920; *The Principle of Relativity*, 1922. All published by the Cambridge University Press.

their place; (2) that the conventional or subjective part in our observation of physical phenomena, though much greater than was formerly supposed, can be eliminated by means of a certain mathematical method known as the tensor calculus. I shall say nothing on this latter topic, as it is intolerably technical.

As regards time, it must be understood, to begin with, that we are not dealing with a philosophical speculation, but with a theory necessitated by experimental results and embodied in mathematical formulae. There is the same sort of difference between the two as there is between the theories of Montesquieu and the American Constitution. What emerges is this: that while the events that happen to a given piece of matter have a definite time-order from the point of view of an observer who shares its motion, events which happen to pieces of matter in different places have not always a definite time-order. To be precise: if a light-signal is sent from the earth to the sun, and reflected back to the earth, it will return to the earth about sixteen minutes after it was sent out. The events which happen on the earth during those sixteen minutes are neither earlier nor later than the arrival of the light-signal at the sun. If we imagine observers moving in all possible ways with respect to the earth and the sun, observing the events on the earth during those sixteen minutes, and also the arrival of the light-signal at the sun; if we assume that all these observers allow for the velocity of light and employ perfectly accurate chronometers; then some of these observers will judge any given event on earth during those sixteen minutes to be earlier than the arrival of the light-signal at the sun, some will judge it to be simultaneous, and some will judge it to be later. All are equally right or equally wrong. From the impersonal standpoint of physics, the events on earth during those sixteen minutes are neither earlier nor later than the arrival of the light-signal at the sun, nor yet simultaneous with it. We cannot say that an event A in one piece of matter is definitely earlier than an event B in another unless light can travel from A to B, starting when the earlier event happens (according to A's time), and arriving before the later event happens (according to B's time). Otherwise the apparent time-order of the two events will vary according to the observer, and will therefore not represent any physical fact.

If velocities comparable with that of light were common in our experience, it is probable that the physical world would have seemed too complicated to be tackled by scientific methods, so that we should have been content with medicine-men down to the present day. But if physics *had* been discovered, it would have had to be the physics of Einstein, because Newtonian physics would have been obviously inapplicable. Radio-active substances send out particles which move very nearly with the velocity of light, and the behaviour of these particles would be unintelligible without the new physics of relativity. There is no doubt that the old physics is faulty, and from a philosophical point of view it is no excuse to say that the fault is 'only a little one'. We have to make up our minds to the fact that, within certain limits, there is no definite time-order between events which happen in different places. This is the fact which has led to the introduction of the single manifold called 'space-time' instead of the two separate manifolds called 'space' and 'time'. The time that we have been regarding as cosmic is really 'local time', a time bound up with the motion of the earth with as little claim to universality as that of a ship which does not alter its clocks in crossing the Atlantic.

When we consider the part that time plays in all our common notions, it becomes evident that our outlook would be profoundly changed if we really imaginatively realised what the physicists have done. Take the notion of 'progress': if the time-order is arbitrary, there will be progress or retrogression according to the convention adopted in measuring time. The notion of distance in space is of course also affected: two observers who employ every possible device for ensuring accuracy will arrive at different estimates of the distance between two places, if the observers are in rapid relative motion. It is obvious that the very idea of distance has become vague, because distance must be between material things, not points of empty space (which are fictions); and it must be the distance at a given time, because the distance between any two bodies is continually changing; and a given time is a subjective notion, dependent upon the way the observer is travelling. We can no longer speak of a body at a given time, but must speak simply of an event. Between two events there is, quite independently of any observer, a certain relation called the 'interval' between them. This interval will be differently analysed by different observers into a spatial and a temporal component, but this analysis has no objective validity. The interval is an objective physical fact, but its separation into spatial and temporal elements is not.

It is obvious that our old comfortable notion of 'solid matter' cannot survive. A piece of matter is nothing but a series of events obeying certain laws. The conception of matter arose at a time when philosophers had no doubts as to the validity of the conception of 'substance'. Matter was substance which was in space and time, mind was substance which was in time only. The notion of substance grew more shadowy in metaphysics as time went on, but it survived in physics because it did no harm – until relativity was invented. Substance, traditionally, was a notion compounded of two elements. First, a substance had the logical property that it could only occur as subject in a proposition, not as predicate. Secondly, it was something that persisted through time, or, in the case of God, was outside time altogether. These two properties had no necessary connection, but this was not perceived because physics taught that bits of matter are immortal and theology taught that the soul is immortal. Both, therefore, were thought to have both the characteristics of substance. Now, however, physics compels us to regard evanescent events as substances in the logical sense, i.e. as subjects which cannot be predicates. A piece of matter, which we took to be a single persistent entity, is really a string of entities, like the apparently persistent objects in a cinema. And there is no reason why we should not say the same of a mind: the persistent ego seems as fictitious as the permanent atom. Both are only strings of events having certain interesting relations to each other.

Modern physics enables us to give body to the suggestion of Mach and James, that the 'stuff' of the mental and physical worlds is the same. 'Solid matter' was obviously very different from thoughts and also from the persistent ego. But if matter and the ego are both only convenient aggregations of events, it is much less difficult to imagine them composed out of the same materials. Moreover, what has hitherto seemed one of the most marked peculiarities of mind, namely subjectivity, or the possession of a point of view, has now invaded physics, and is found not to involve mind: photographic cameras in different places may photograph the 'same' event, but they will photograph it differently. Even chronometers and measuring-rods become subjective in modern physics; what they directly record is not a physical fact, but their relation to a physical fact. Thus physics and psychology have approached each other, and the old dualism of mind and matter has broken down.

It is perhaps worthwhile to point out that modern physics knows nothing of 'force' in the old or popular sense of that word. We used to think that the sun exerted a 'force' on the earth. Now we think that space-time, in the neighbourhood of the sun, is so shaped that the earth finds it less trouble to move as it does than in any other way. The great principle of modern physics is the 'principle of least action', that in going from one place to another a body always chooses the route which involves least action. (Action is a technical term, but its meaning need not concern us at present.) Newspapers and certain writers who wish to be thought forceful are fond of the word 'dynamic'. There is nothing 'dynamic' in dynamics, which, on the contrary, finds everything deducible from a law of universal laziness. And there is no such thing as one body 'controlling' the movements of another. The universe of modern science is much more like that of Lao-Tze than that of those who prate of 'great laws' and 'natural forces'.

The modern philosophy of pluralism and realism has, in some ways, less to offer than earlier philosophies. In the Middle Ages, philosophy was the handmaid of theology; to this day, they come under one heading in booksellers' catalogues. It has been generally regarded as the business of philosophy to prove the great truths of religion. The new realism does not profess to be able to prove them, or even to disprove them. It aims only at clarifying the fundamental ideas of the sciences, and synthesising the different sciences in a single comprehensive view of that fragment of the world that science has succeeded in exploring. It does not know what lies beyond; it possesses no talisman for transforming ignorance into knowledge. It offers intellectual delights to those who value them, but it does not attempt to flatter human conceit as most philosophies do. If it is dry and technical, it lays the blame on the universe, which has chosen to work in a mathematical way rather than as poets or mystics might have desired. Perhaps this is regrettable, but a mathematician can hardly be expected to regret it.

Chapter 6

Machines and the Emotions

Will machines destroy emotions, or will emotions destroy machines? This question was suggested long ago by Samuel Butler in *Erewhon*, but it is growing more and more actual as the empire of machinery is enlarged.

At first sight, it is not obvious why there should be any opposition between machines and emotions. Every normal boy loves machines; the bigger and more powerful they are, the more he loves them. Nations which have a long tradition of artistic excellence, like the Japanese, are captivated by Western mechanical methods as soon as they come across them, and long only to imitate us as quickly as possible. Nothing annoys an educated and travelled Asiatic so much as to hear praise of 'the wisdom of the East' or the traditional virtues of Asiatic civilisation. He feels as a boy would feel who was told to play with dolls instead of toy automobiles. And like a boy, he would prefer a real automobile to a toy one, not realising that it may run over him.

In the West, when machinery was new, there was the same delight in it, except on the part of a few poets and aesthetes. The nineteenth century considered itself superior to its predecessors chiefly because of its mechanical progress. Peacock, in its early years, makes fun of the 'steam intellect society', because he is a literary man, to whom the Greek and Latin authors represent civilisation; but he is conscious of being out of touch with the prevailing tendencies of his time. Rousseau's disciples with the return to Nature, the Lake Poets with their mediaevalism, William Morris with his *News from Nowhere* (a country where it is always June and everybody is engaged in haymaking), all represent a purely sentimental and essentially reactionary opposition to machinery. Samuel Butler was the first man to apprehend intellectually the non-sentimental case against machines, but in him it may have been no more than a *jeu d'esprit* – certainly it was not a deeply held conviction. Since his day numbers of people in the most mechanised nations have been tending to adopt in earnest a view similar to that of the Erewhonians; this view, that is to say, has been latent or explicit in the attitude of many rebels against existing industrial methods.

Machines are worshipped because they are beautiful, and valued because they confer power; they are hated because they are hideous, and loathed because they impose slavery. Do not let us suppose that one of these attitudes is 'right' and the other 'wrong', any more than it would be right to maintain that men have heads but wrong to maintain that they have feet, though we can easily imagine Lilliputians disputing this question concerning Gulliver. A machine is like a Djinn in the Arabian Nights: beautiful and beneficent to its master; but hideous and terrible to his enemies. But in our day nothing is allowed to show itself with such naked simplicity. The master of the machine, it is true, lives at a distance from it, where he cannot hear its noise or see its unsightly heaps of slag or smell its noxious fumes; if he ever sees it, the occasion is before it is installed in use, when he can admire its force or its delicate precision without being troubled by dust and heat. But when he is challenged to consider the machine from the point of view of those who have to live with it and work it, he has a ready answer. He can point out that, owing to its operations, these men can purchase more goods – often vastly more – than their great-grandfathers could. It follows that they must be happier than their great-grandfathers – if we are to accept an assumption which is made by almost everyone.

The assumption is, that the possession of material commodities is what makes men happy. It is thought that a man who has two rooms and two beds and two loaves must be twice as happy as a man who has one room and one bed and one loaf. In a word, it is thought that happiness is proportional to income. A few people, not always quite sincerely, challenge this idea in the name of religion or morality; but they are glad if they increase their income by the eloquence of their preaching. It is not from a moral or religious point of view that I wish to challenge it; it is from the point of view of psychology and observation of life. If happiness is proportional to income, the case for machinery is unanswerable; if not the whole question remains to be examined.

Men have physical needs, and they have emotions. While physical needs are unsatisfied, they take first place; but when they are satisfied, emotions unconnected with them become important in deciding whether a man is to be happy or unhappy. In modern industrial communities there are many men, women and children whose bare physical needs are not adequately supplied; as regards them, I do not deny that the first requisite for happiness is an increase of income. But they are a minority, and it would not be difficult to give the bare necessaries of life to all of them. It is not of them that I wish to speak, but of those who have more than is necessary to support existence – not only those who have much more, but also those who have only a little more.

Why do we, in fact, almost all of us, desire to increase our incomes? It may seem, at first sight, as though material goods were what we desire. But, in fact, we desire these mainly in order to impress our neighbours. When a man moves into a larger house in a more genteel quarter, he reflects that 'better' people will call on his wife, and some unprosperous cronies of former days can be dropped. When he sends his son to a good school or an expensive university, he consoles himself for the heavy fees by thoughts of the social kudos to be gained. In every big city, whether of Europe or of America, houses in some districts are more expensive than equally good houses in other districts, merely because they are more fashionable. One of the most powerful of all our passions is the desire to be admired and respected. As things stand, admiration and respect are given to the man who seems to be rich. This is the chief reason why people wish to be rich. The actual goods purchased by their money play quite a secondary part. Take, for example, a millionaire who cannot tell one picture from another, but has acquired a gallery of old masters by the help of experts. The only pleasure he derives from his pictures is the thought that others know how much they have cost; he could derive more direct enjoyment from sentimental chromos out of Christmas numbers, but he would not obtain the same satisfaction for his vanity.

All this might be different, and has been different in many societies. In aristocratic epochs, men have been admired for their birth. In some circles in Paris, men are admired for their artistic or literary excellence, strange as it may seem. In a German university, a man may actually be admired for his learning. In India saints are admired; in China, sages. The study of these differing societies shows the correctness of our analysis, for in all of them we find a large percentage of men who are indifferent to money so long as they have enough to keep alive on, but are keenly desirous of the merits by which, in their environment, respect is to be won.

The importance of these facts lies in this, that the modern desire for wealth is not inherent in human nature, and could be destroyed by different social institutions. If, by law, we all had exactly the same income, we should have to seek some other way of being superior to our neighbours, and most of our present craving for material possessions would cease. Moreover, since this craving is in the nature of a competition, it only brings happiness when we outdistance a rival, to whom it brings correlative pain. A general increase of wealth gives no competitive advantage, and therefore brings no competitive happiness. There is, of course, *some* pleasure derived from the actual enjoyment of goods purchased, but, as we have seen, this is a very small part of what makes us desire wealth. And in so far as our desire is competitive, no increase of human happiness as a whole comes from increase of wealth, whether general or particular.

If we are to argue that machinery increases happiness, therefore, the increase of material prosperity which it brings cannot weigh very heavily in its favour, except in so far as it may be used to prevent absolute destitution. But there is no inherent reason why it should be so used. Destitution can be prevented without machinery where the population is stationary; of this France may serve as an example, since there is very little destitution and much less machinery than in America, England, or pre-war Germany. Conversely, there may be much destitution where there is much machinery; of this we have examples in the industrial areas of England a hundred years ago and of Japan at the present day. The prevention of destitution does not depend upon machines, but upon quite other factors – partly density of population, and partly political conditions. And apart from prevention of destitution, the value of increasing wealth is not very great.

Meanwhile, machines deprive us of two things which are certainly important ingredients of human happiness, namely, spontaneity and variety. Machines have their own pace, and their own insistent demands: a man who has expensive plant must keep it working. The great trouble with the machine, from the point of view of the emotions, is its *regularity*. And, of course, conversely, the great objection to the emotions, from the point of view of the machine, is their *irregularity*. As the machine dominates the thoughts of people who consider themselves 'serious', the highest praise they can give to a man is to suggest that he has the qualities of a machine – that he is reliable, punctual, exact, etc. And an 'irregular' life has come to be synonymous with a bad life. Against this point of view Bergson's philosophy was a protest – not, to my mind, wholly sound from an intellectual point of view, but inspired by a wholesome dread of seeing men turned more and more into machines.

In life, as opposed to thought, the rebellion of our instincts against enslavement to mechanism has hitherto taken a most unfortunate direction. The impulse to war has always existed since men took to living in societies, but it did not, in the past have the same intensity or virulence as it has in our day. In the eighteenth century, England and France had innumerable wars, and contended for the hegemony of the world; but they liked and respected each other the whole time. Officer prisoners joined in the social life of their captors, and were honoured guests at their dinner-parties. At the beginning of our war with Holland in 1665, a man came home from Africa with atrocity stories about the Dutch there; we [the British] persuaded ourselves that his story was false, punished him, and published the Dutch denial. In the late war we should have knighted him, and imprisoned anyone who threw doubt on his veracity. The greater ferocity of modern war is attributable to machines, which operate in three different ways. First, they make it possible to have larger armies. Secondly, they facilitate a cheap Press, which flourishes by appealing to men's baser passions. Thirdly – and this is the point that concerns us – they starve the anarchic, spontaneous side of human nature, which works underground, producing an obscure discontent, to which the thought of war appeals as affording possible relief. It is a mistake to attribute a vast upheaval like the late war merely to the machinations of politicians. In Russia, perhaps, such an explanation would have been adequate; that is one reason why Russia fought half-heartedly, and made a revolution to secure peace. But in England, Germany and the United States (in 1917), no Government could have withstood the popular demand for war. A popular demand of this sort must have an instinctive basis, and for my part I believe that the modern increase in warlike instinct is attributable to the dissatisfaction (mostly unconscious) caused by the regularity, monotony and tameness of modern life.

It is obvious that we cannot deal with this situation by abolishing machinery. Such a measure would be reactionary, and is in any case impracticable. The only way of avoiding the evils at present associated with machinery is to provide breaks in the monotony, with every encouragement to high adventure during the intervals. Many men would cease to desire war if they had opportunities to risk their lives in Alpine climbing; one of the ablest and most vigorous workers for peace that it has been my good fortune to know habitually spent his summer climbing the most dangerous peaks in the Alps. If every working man had a month in the year during which, if he chose, he could be taught to work an aeroplane, or encouraged to hunt for sapphires in the Sahara, or otherwise enabled to engage in some dangerous and exciting pursuit involving quick personal initiative, the popular love of war would become confined to women and invalids. I confess I know no method of making these classes pacific, but I am convinced that a scientific psychology would find a method if it undertook the task in earnest.

Machines have altered our way of life, but not our instincts. Consequently there is maladjustment. The whole psychology of the emotions and instincts is as yet in its infancy; a beginning has been made by psycho-analysis, but only a beginning. What we may accept from psycho-analysis is the fact that people will, in action, pursue various ends which they do not *consciously* desire, and will have an attendant set of quite irrational beliefs which enable them to pursue these ends without knowing that they are doing so. But orthodox psycho-analysis has unduly simplified our unconscious purposes, which are numerous, and differ from one person to another. It is to be hoped that social and political phenomena will soon come to be understood from this point of view, and will thus throw light on average human nature.

Moral self-control, and external prohibition of harmful acts, are not adequate methods of dealing with our anarchic instincts. The reason they are inadequate is that these instincts are capable of as many disguises as the Devil in mediaeval legend, and some of these disguises deceive even the elect. The only adequate method is to discover what are the needs of our instinctive nature, and then to search for the least harmful way of satisfying them. Since spontaneity is what is most thwarted by machines, the only thing that can be *provided* is opportunity; the use made of opportunity must be left to the initiative of the individual. No doubt considerable expense would be involved; but it would not be comparable to the expense of war. Understanding of human nature must be the basis of any real improvement in human life. Science has done wonders in mastering the laws of the physical world, but our own nature is much less understood, as yet, than the nature of stars and electrons. When science learns to understand human nature, it will be able to bring a happiness into our lives which machines and the physical sciences have failed to create.

Chapter 7

Behaviourism and Values

In an American learned periodical I once found the statement that there is only one behaviourist in the world, namely Dr Watson. I should have said there are as many as there are modern-minded men. This is not to say that behaviourists are common in universities, nor yet that I am myself a behaviourist – for, ever since the year in which I saw Russia and China, I have realised that I am not up to date. Objective self-criticism, however, compels me to admit that it would be better if I were. In this essay I want to set forth certain difficulties which are felt by persons like myself, who, while accepting what is modern in science, have difficulty in divesting themselves of mediaevalism as regards what is worth living for. I want to ask, not only what is the logical bearing of behaviourism upon values, but what is likely to be its effect upon ordinary men and women if widely accepted in a necessarily crude form. It has not yet become a craze, like psycho-analysis; but if it ever does, its popular form will no doubt differ greatly from Dr Watson's teaching – as greatly as popular Freudianism does from Freud.

The popular version of behaviourism will, I imagine, be something like this: In old days there was supposed to be a thing called the mind, which was capable of three types of activity, feeling, knowing and willing. Now, it has been ascertained that there is no such thing as the mind, but only the body. All our activities consist of bodily processes. 'Feeling' consists of visceral occurrences, particularly such as are connected with the glands. 'Knowing' consists of movements of the larynx. 'Willing' consists of all other movements depending upon striped muscles. When, recently, a famous intellectual married a famous dancer, there were some who expressed doubt as to their congruity. But from a behaviourist standpoint such a doubt was misplaced: she had cultivated the muscles of legs and arms, he the muscles of the larynx, so that both were acrobats, though belonging to different branches of the profession.

Since the only thing we can do is to move our bodies, the popular votaries of the creed are likely to infer that we ought to move them as much as possible. At this point difficulties will arise as regards relativity. Should the different parts of the body move relatively to each other? Or should the body as a whole move relatively to the vehicle in which it finds itself? Or is motion relative to the earth the criterion of virtue? The ideal man on the first view is the acrobat; on the second, the man who runs up an escalator which is coming down; on the third, the man who spends his life in an aeroplane. It is not easy to see on what principle the resulting controversies are to be decided, but on the whole I back the aeronauts.

When we consider the conceptions of human excellence which dominate the most powerful sections of the most powerful countries, we are led to the conclusion that behaviourism merely supplies a theoretical justification for what is already believed. The acrobat should be the ideal of those who believe in physical culture and hold that a nation's manhood depends upon its athletics, which is the prevalent view in the British governing class. The man who went up a descending escalator should be the *beau idéal* of the muscular Christians, who regard the development of muscle as the ultimate good, provided it can be divorced from pleasure. This is the view which the YMCA endeavours to inculcate in China, and which our rulers regard as appropriate to all subject races and classes. The aeronaut represents a more aristocratic ideal, reserved for those who exercise mechanical power. But, over and above all these, there is a supreme conception, which suggests Aristotle's unmoved mover; it is that of the ruler at rest in the centre, while all else revolves round him at varying rates, thus securing for him the absolute maximum of *relative* motion. This role is reserved for our supermen, especially financiers.

Now there is a quite different conception of human excellence which has come down to us from Greece and the Middle Ages, but is being gradually displaced by the outlook due to the domination of machines over the imagination. I believe this older outlook to be logically reconcilable with behaviourism, but not *psychologically* in the behaviour of the average citizen. In this older outlook, feeling and knowing are considered as important as doing; art and contemplation are thought to be as admirable as altering the positions in space of large quantities of matter. The Cherubim love

God and the Seraphim contemplate Him, and in this consists their supreme excellence. The whole ideal is static. It is true that in heaven hymns are sung and harps are played, but they are the same hymns every day, and no improvement in the construction of harps is tolerated. Such an existence bores the modern man. One reason why theology has lost its hold is that it has failed to provide progressive machinery in heaven, though Milton provided it in hell.

It may be laid down that every ethical system is based upon a certain *non sequitur*. The philosopher first invents a false theory as to the nature of things, and then deduces that wicked actions are those which show that his theory is false. To begin with the traditional Christian: he argues that, since everything always obeys the will of God, wickedness consists in disobedience to the will of God. We then come on to the Hegelian, who argues that the universe consists of parts which harmonise in a perfect organism, and therefore wickedness consists of behaviour which diminishes the harmony – though it is difficult to see how such behaviour is possible, since complete harmony is metaphysically necessary. Bergson, writing for a French public, holds a threat over those whose acts refute him which is even more terrible than moral condemnation – I mean, the thread of ridicule. He shows that human beings never behave mechanically, and then, in his book on *Laughter,* he argues that what makes us laugh is to see a person behaving mechanically, i.e. you are ridiculous when you do something that shows Bergson's philosophy to be false, and only then. These examples have, I hope, made it plain that a metaphysic can never have ethical consequences except in virtue of its falsehood: if it were true, the acts which it defines as sin would be impossible.

Applying these remarks to behaviourism, I deduce that if, and in so far as, it has ethical consequences, it must be false, while conversely, if it is true, it can have no bearing in conduct. Applying this test to popular behaviourism (though not to the strictly scientific form), I find several evidences of falsehood. In the first place, almost all its votaries would lose all interest in it if they thought it had no ethical consequences. Now at this point it is necessary to draw a distinction. A true doctrine may have *practical* consequences, though it cannot have *ethical* consequences. If you attempt to extract things from an automatic machine by means of one coin, when it is constructed to require two, the truth has a *practical* consequence, namely that you must offer it another coin. But no one would call this consequence 'ethical'; it merely has to do with how to realise your desires. Similarly, behaviourism, as developed in Dr Watson's book with that title, has undoubtedly all sorts of important practical consequences, particularly in education. If you want a child to learn to behave in a certain way, you will often be wise if you follow Dr Watson's advice rather than (say) Freud's. But this is a scientific matter, not an ethical matter; ethics only comes in when it is said that action ought to have certain ends in view, or (alternatively) that certain actions can be classified as good or bad independently of their consequences.

Now I find that behaviourism does tend, however illogically, to have an ethic in the proper sense of the word. The argument seems to be: since the only thing we can do is to cause matter to move, we ought to move as much matter as possible; consequently art and thought are valuable only in so far as they stimulate the motions of matter. This, however, is too metaphysical a criterion for daily life; the practical criterion is income. Take the following from Dr Watson:

'In my opinion, one of the most important elements in the judging of personality, character and ability, is the history of the individual's yearly achievements. We can measure this objectively by the length of time the individual stayed in his various positions and the yearly increases he received in his earnings. ... If the individual is a writer, we should want to draw a curve of the prices he gets for his stories year by year. If from our leading magazines he receives the same average price per word for his stories at thirty that he received at twenty-four, the chances are he is a hack writer, and will never do anything but that.'

Applying this criterion to Buddha, Christ and Mahomet, to Milton and Blake, we see that it involves an interesting readjustment in our estimates of the values of personalities. In addition to points already noted, there are two ethical maxims implicit in this passage. One is that excellence must be easily measurable, the other that it must consist in conformity to law. These are both natural consequences of the attempt to deduce ethics from a system based upon physics. For my part, the ethic suggested by the above passage from Dr Watson is not one that I can accept. I cannot believe that virtue is proportional to income, nor yet that it is wicked to have difficulty in conforming to the herd. Doubtless my views on these matters are biased, since I am poor and a crank; but although I recognise this fact, they remain my views none the less.

I will now take another aspect of behaviourism, namely its views on education. Here I cannot cite Dr Watson, whose views on the subject, so far as they appear in his works, seem to me excellent. But he does not deal with the later parts of education, and it is there that my doubts are strongest. I will take a book which, while not explicitly behaviouristic, is, in fact, largely inspired by the outlook with which behaviourism is connected, I mean: *The Child: His Nature and His Needs*.[1] This is a book for which, in the main, I have the highest respect, because its psychology is admirable; but its ethics and aesthetics seem to me more open to criticism. To illustrate the aesthetic lack, I take the following passage (p. 384):

'Twenty-five years ago pupils learned to spell from ten to fifteen thousand words; but as a result of investigations carried on during the past two decades, it has been found that the typical graduate of a high school does not need in his school work, and will not need in later life, to spell more than three thousand words at the outside, unless he engages in some technical pursuit, when it may be necessary for him to master a special and technical vocabulary. The typical American in his correspondence and in his writing for the newspaper rarely employs more than fifteen hundred different words; many of us never use more than half this number. In view of these facts, the course in spelling in the schools today is being constructed on the principle that the words that will actually be used in daily life should be mastered so that they can be spelled automatically, and the technical and unusual words that were formerly taught but will probably never be used are being eliminated. Not a single word is being retained in present-day spelling courses on the theory that it will be valuable in the training of memory.'

[1] Prepared under the editorial supervision of M. V. O'Shea, Professor of Education in the University of Wisconsin. A contribution of the Children's Foundation.

In the last sentence we have a perfectly sound appeal to psychology in refutation of a former argument in favour of memorising. It appears that memorising does not train the memory; therefore nothing should be memorised on any ground except that just that fact should be known. That granted, let us examine the other implications of the above passage.

In the first place, there is no point whatever in being able to spell anything. Shakespeare and Milton could not spell; Marie Corelli and Alfred Austen could. Spelling is thought desirable partly for snobbish reasons, as an easy way of distinguishing the 'educated' from the 'uneducated'; partly, like correct clothes, as a part of herd domination; partly because the devotee of natural law feels pain in the spectacle of any sphere in which individual liberty remains. If it is thought that print, at least, ought to be spelled conventionally, it is always possible to keep readers for the purpose.

In the second place, the written language, except in China, is representative of the spoken language, in which resides the whole aesthetic quality of literature. In the days when men retained the feeling that language could and should be beautiful, they were careless of spelling, but careful of pronunciation. Now, even persons of university education do not know how to pronounce any but the commonest words, and are consequently unable to scan a great deal of poetry. Apart from professional students of literature, there is probably hardly a single person under forty in America who can scan—

> Scattering unbeholden
> Its aerial hue.

Instead of being taught to spell, children ought to be taught to read aloud, if any care for aesthetic considerations existed in education. Formerly the paterfamilias read the Bible aloud, which served admirably for this purpose; but now this practice has become almost extinct.

Not only is it important to know pronunciation, but it is also desirable aesthetically to have a large vocabulary. Those who know only fifteen hundred words will be unable to express themselves with either precision or beauty except on simple topics and by rare good luck. About half the population of America at the present time spends as much time on its education as Shakespeare spent, but its vocabulary is hardly a tenth of his. Yet his must have been intelligible to the ordinary citizen of his time, since it was used in plays which had to be a commercial success. The modern view is that a man has enough command of language if he can make himself understood; the older view was that both in speech and in writing he should be able to give aesthetic pleasure.

What is the conclusion for a person who, like the present writer, accepts, for practical purposes, the scientific part of behaviourism, while rejecting the supposed ethical and aesthetic consequences? I have the highest admiration for Dr Watson, and consider his books enormously important. I consider that, at the present time, physics is the most important of theoretical pursuits, and industrialism is the most important sociological phenomenon. Nevertheless, I cannot cease to admire 'useless' knowledge, and art which has no purpose except to give delight. The problem is not logical; for, as we have seen, if behaviourism is true it can have no bearing upon questions of value, except in the subordinate way of helping to show what means to use for a given end. The problem is, in a broad sense, political: given that the bulk of mankind are certain to commit fallacies, is it better that they should deduce false conclusions from true premisses or true conclusions from false premisses? A question of this sort is insoluble. The only true solution seems to be that ordinary men and women should be taught logic, so as to be able to refrain from drawing conclusions which only *seem* to follow. When it is said, for example, that the French are 'logical', what is meant is that, when they accept a premiss, they also accept everything that a person totally destitute of logical subtlety would erroneously suppose to follow from the premiss. This is a most undesirable quality, from which, on the whole, the English-speaking nations have, in the past, been more free than any others. But there are signs that, if they are to remain free in this respect, they will require more philosophy and logic than they have had in the past. Logic was, formerly, the art of drawing inferences; it has now become the art of abstaining from inferences, since it has appeared that the inferences we feel naturally inclined to make are hardly ever valid. I conclude, therefore, that logic ought to be taught in schools with a view to teaching people not to reason. For, if they reason, they will almost certainly reason wrongly.

Chapter 8

Eastern and Western Ideals of Happiness

Everybody knows Wells's Time Machine, which enabled its possessor to travel backward or forward in time, and see for himself what the past was like and what the future will be. But people do not always realise that a great deal of the advantages of Wells's device can be secured by travelling about the world at the present day. A European who goes to New York and Chicago sees the future, the future to which Europe is likely to come if it escapes economic disaster. On the other hand, when he goes to Asia he sees the past. In India, I am told, he can see the Middle Ages; in China he can see[1] the eighteenth century. If George Washington were to return to earth, the country which he created would puzzle him dreadfully. He would feel a little less strange in England, still less strange in France; but he would not feel really at home until he reached China. There, for the first time in his ghostly wanderings, he would find men who still believe in 'life, liberty and the pursuit of happiness', and who conceive these things more or less as Americans of the War of Independence conceived them. And I think it would not be long before he became President of the Chinese Republic.

Western civilisation embraces North and South America, Europe excluding Russia, and the British self-governing dominions. In this civilisation the United States leads the van; all the characteristics that distinguish the West from the East are most marked and farthest developed in America. We are accustomed to take progress for granted: to assume without hesitation that the changes which have happened during the last hundred years were unquestionably for the better, and that further changes for the better are sure to follow indefinitely. On the Continent of Europe, the war and its consequences have administered a blow to this

[1] 1920.

confident belief, and men have begun to look back to the time before 1914 as a golden age, not likely to recur for centuries. In England there has been much less of this shock to optimism, and in America still less. For those of us who have been accustomed to take progress for granted, it is especially interesting to visit a country like China, which has remained where we were one hundred and fifty years ago, and to ask ourselves whether, on the balance, the changes which have happened to us have brought any real improvement.

The civilisation of China, as every one knows, is based upon the teaching of Confucius, who flourished five hundred years before Christ. Like the Greeks and Romans, he did not think of human society as naturally progressive; on the contrary, he believed that in remote antiquity rulers had been wise, and the people had been happy to a degree which the degenerate present could admire but hardly achieve. This, of course, was a delusion. But the practical result was that Confucius, like other teachers of antiquity, aimed at creating a stable society, maintaining a certain level of excellence, but not always striving after new successes. In this he was more successful than any other man who ever lived. His personality has been stamped on Chinese civilisation from his day to our own. During his lifetime the Chinese occupied only a small part of present-day China, and were divided into a number of warring states. During the next three hundred years they established themselves throughout what is now China proper, and founded an empire exceeding in territory and population any other that existed until the last fifty years. In spite of barbarian invasions, Mongol and Manchu dynasties, and occasional longer or shorter periods of chaos and civil war, the Confucian system survived, bringing with it art and literature and a civilised way of life. It is only in our own day, through contact with the West and with the westernised Japanese, that this system has begun to break down.

A system which has had this extraordinary power of survival must have great merits, and certainly deserves our respect and consideration. It is not a religion, as we understand the word, because it is not associated with the supernatural or with mystical beliefs. It is a purely ethical system, but its ethics, unlike those of Christianity, are not too exalted for ordinary men to practise. In essence, what Confucius teaches is something very like the old-fashioned ideal of a 'gentleman' as it existed in the eighteenth century. One of his sayings will illustrate this (I quote from Lionel Giles's *Sayings of Confucius*):

'The true gentleman is never contentious. If a spirit of rivalry is anywhere unavoidable, it is at a shooting-match. Yet even here he courteously salutes his opponents before taking up his position, and again when, having lost, he retires to drink the forfeit-cup. So that even when competing he remains a true gentleman.'

He speaks much, as a moral teacher is bound to do, about duty and virtue and such matters, but he never exacts anything contrary to nature and the natural affections. This is shown in the following conversation:

'The Duke of She addressed Confucious, saying: We have an upright man in our country. His father stole a sheep, and the son bore witness against him. – In our country, Confucius replied, uprightness is something different from this. A father hides the guilt of his son, and a son hides the guilt of his father. It is in such conduct that true uprightness is to be found.'

Confucius was in all things moderate, even in virtue. He did not believe that we ought to return good for evil. He was asked on one occasion: 'How do you regard the principle of returning good for evil?' And he replied: 'What, then, is to be the return for good? Rather should you return justice for injustice, and good for good.' The principle of returning good for evil was being taught in his day in China by the Taoists, whose teaching is much more akin to that of Christianity than is the teaching of Confucius. The founder of Taoism, Lao-Tze (supposed to have been an older contemporary of Confucius), says: 'To the good I would be good; to the not-good I would also be good, in order to make them good. With the faithful I would keep faith; with the unfaithful I would also keep faith, in order that they may become faithful. Even if a man is bad, how can it be right to cast him off? Requite injury with kindness.' Some of Lao-Tze's words are amazingly like parts of the Sermon on the Mount. For instance, he says:

'He that humbles himself shall be preserved entire. He that bends shall be made straight. He that is empty shall be filled. He that is worn out shall be renewed. He who has little shall succeed. He who has much shall go astray.'

It is characteristic of China that it was not Lao-Tze but Confucius who became the recognised national sage. Taoism has survived, but chiefly as magic and among the uneducated. Its doctrines have appeared visionary to the practical men who administered the Empire, while the doctrines of Confucius were eminently calculated to avoid friction. Lao-Tze preached a doctrine of inaction: 'The empire,' he says, 'has ever been won by letting things take their course. He who must always be doing is unfit to obtain the empire.' But Chinese governors naturally preferred the Confucian maxims of self-control, benevolence and courtesy, combined, as they were, with a great emphasis upon the good that could be done by wise government. It never occurred to the Chinese, as it has to all modern white nations, to have one system of ethics in theory and another in practice. I do not mean that they always live up to their own theories, but that they attempt to do so and are expected to do so, whereas there are large parts of the Christian ethic which are universally admitted to be too good for this wicked world.

We have, in fact, two kinds of morality side by side: one which we preach but do not practise, and another which we practise but seldom preach. Christianity, like all religions except Mormonism, is Asiatic in origin; it had in the early centuries that emphasis on individualism and other-worldliness which is characteristic of Asiatic mysticism. From this point of view, the doctrine of non-resistance was intelligible. But when Christianity became the nominal religion of energetic European princes, it was found necessary to maintain that some texts were not to be taken literally, while others, such as 'render unto Caesar the things that are Caesar's', acquired great popularity. In our own day, under the influence of competitive industrialism, the slightest approach to non-resistence is despised, and men are expected to be able to keep their end up. In practice, our effective morality is that of material success achieved by means of a struggle; and this applies to nations as well as to individuals. Anything else seems to us soft and foolish.

The Chinese do not adopt either our theoretical or our practical ethic. They admit in theory that there are occasions when it is proper to fight, and in practice that these occasions are rare; whereas we hold in theory that there are no occasions when it is proper to fight and in practice that such occasions are very frequent. The Chinese sometimes fight, but are not a combative race, and do not greatly admire success in war or in business. Traditionally, they admire learning more than anything else; next to that, and usually in combination with it, they admire urbanity and courtesy. For ages past, administrative posts have been awarded in China on the results of competitive examinations. As there has been no hereditary aristocracy for two thousand years – with the sole exception of the family of Confucius, the head of which is a Duke – learning has drawn to itself the kind of respect which, in feudal Europe, was given to powerful nobles, as well as the respect which it inspired on its own account. The old learning, however, was very narrow, consisting merely in an uncritical study of the Chinese classics and their recognised commentators. Under the influence of the West, it has come to be known that geography, economics, geology, chemistry and so on, are of more practical use than the moralisings of former ages. Young China – that is to say, the students who have been educated on European lines – recognise modern needs, and have perhaps hardly enough respect for the old tradition. Nevertheless, even the most modern, with few exceptions, retain the traditional virtues of moderation, politeness and a pacific temper. Whether these virtues will survive a few more decades of Western and Japanese tuition is perhaps doubtful.

If I were to try to sum up in a phrase the main difference between the Chinese and ourselves, I should say that they, in the main, aim at enjoyment, while we, in the main, aim at power. We like power over our fellow-men, and we like power over Nature. For the sake of the former we have built up strong states, and for the sake of the latter we have built up Science. The Chinese are too lazy and too good-natured for such pursuits. To say that they are lazy is, however, only true in a certain sense. They are not lazy in the way that Russians are, that is to say, they will work hard for their living. Employers of labour find them extraordinarily industrious. But they will not work, as Americans and Western Europeans do, simply because they would be bored if they did not work, nor do they love hustle for its own sake. When they have enough to live on, they live on it, instead of trying to augment it by hard work. They have an infinite capacity for leisurely amusements – going to the theatre, talking while they drink tea, admiring the Chinese art of earlier times, or walking in beautiful scenery. To our way of thinking, there is something unduly mild about such a way of spending one's life; we respect more a man who goes to his office every day, even if all that he does in his office is harmful.

Living in the East has, perhaps a corrupting influence upon a white man, but I must confess that, since I came to know China, I have regarded laziness as one of the best qualities of which men in the mass are capable. We achieve certain things by being energetic, but it may be questioned whether, on the balance, the things that we achieve are of any value. We develop wonderful skill in manufacture, part of which we devote to making ships, automobiles, telephones and other means of living luxuriously at high pressure, while another part is devoted to making guns, poison gases and aeroplanes for the purpose of killing each other wholesale. We have a first-class system of administration and taxation, part of which is devoted to education, sanitation and such useful objects, while the rest is devoted to war. In England at the present day most of the national revenue is spent on past and future wars and only the residue on useful objects. On the Continent, in most countries, the proportion is even worse. We have a police system of unexampled efficiency, part of which is devoted to the detection and prevention of crime and part to imprisoning anybody who has any new constructive political ideas. In China, until recently, they had none of these things. Industry was too inefficient to produce either automobiles or bombs; the State too inefficient to educate its own citizens or to kill those of other countries; the police too inefficient to catch either bandits or Bolsheviks. The result was that in China, as compared to any white man's country, there was freedom for all, and a degree of diffused happiness which was amazing in view of the poverty of all but a tiny minority.

Comparing the actual outlook of the average Chinese with that of the average Western, two differences strike one: first, that the Chinese do not admire activity unless it serves some useful purpose; secondly, that they do not regard morality as consisting in checking our own impulses and interfering with those of others. The first of these differences has been already discussed, but the second is perhaps equally important. Professor Giles, the eminent

Chinese scholar, at the end of his Gifford Lectures on 'Confucianism and its Rivals', maintains that the chief obstacle to the
success of Christian missions in China has been the doctrine of
original sin. The traditional doctrine of orthodox Christianity –
still preached by most Christian missionaries in the Far East – is
that we are all born wicked, so wicked as to deserve eternal punishment. The Chinese might have no difficulty in accepting this
doctrine if it applied only to white men, but when they are told
that their own parents and grandparents are in hell-fire they grow
indignant. Confucius taught that men are born good, and that if
they become wicked, that is through the force of evil example or
corrupting manners. This difference from traditional Western
orthodoxy has a profound influence on the outlook of the Chinese.

Among ourselves, the people who are regarded as moral
luminaries are those who forgo ordinary pleasures themselves
and find compensation in interfering with the pleasures of others.
There is an element of the busybody in our conception of virtue:
unless a man makes himself a nuisance to a great many people, we
do not think he can be an exceptionally good man. This attitude
comes from our notion of Sin. It leads not only to interference
with freedom, but also to hypocrisy, since the conventional standard is too difficult for most people to live up to. In China this is
not the case. Moral precepts are positive rather than negative. A
man is expected to be respectful to his parents, kind to his children, generous to his poor relations, and courteous to all. These are
not very difficult duties, but most men actually fulfil them, and the
result is perhaps better than that of our higher standard, from
which most people fall short.

Another result of the absence of the notion of Sin is that men
are much more willing to submit their differences to argument and
reason than they are in the West. Among ourselves, differences of
opinion quickly become questions of 'principle': each side thinks
that the other side is wicked, and that any yielding to it involves
sharing in its guilt. This makes our disputes bitter, and involves in
practice a great readiness to appeal to force. In China, although
there were military men who were ready to appeal to force, no one
took them seriously, not even their own soldiers. They fought
battles which were nearly bloodless, and they did much less harm
than we should expect from our experience of the fiercer conflicts
of the West. The great bulk of the population, including the civil

administration, went about its business as though these generals and their armies did not exist. In ordinary life, disputes are usually adjusted by the friendly mediation of some third party. Compromise is the accepted principle, because it is necessary to save the face of both parties. Saving face, though in some forms it makes foreigners smile, is a most valuable national institution, making social and political life far less ruthless than it is with us.

There is one serious defect, and only one, in the Chinese system, and that is, that it does not enable China to resist more pugnacious nations. If the whole world were like China, the whole world could be happy; but so long as others are warlike and energetic, the Chinese, now that they are no longer isolated, will be compelled to copy our vices to some degree if they are to preserve their national independence. But let us not flatter ourselves that this imitation will be an improvement.

Chapter 9

The Harm That Good Men Do

A hundred years ago there lived a philosopher named Jeremy Bentham, who was universally recognised to be a very wicked man. I remember to this day the first time that I came across his name when I was a boy. It was in a statement by the Rev. Sydney Smith to the effect that Bentham thought people ought to make soup of their dead grandmothers. This practice appeared to me as undesirable from a culinary as from a moral point of view, and I therefore conceived a bad opinion of Bentham. Long afterwards, I discovered that the statement was one of those reckless lies in which respectable people are wont to indulge in the interests of virtue. I also discovered what was the really serious charge against him. It was no less than this: that he defined a 'good' man as a man who does good. This definition, as the reader will perceive at once if he is right-minded, is subversive of all true morality. How much more exalted is the attitude of Kant, who lays it down that a kind action is not virtuous if it springs from affection for the beneficiary, but only if it is inspired by the moral law, which is, of course, just as likely to inspire unkind actions. We know that the exercise of virtue should be its own reward, and it seems to follow that the enduring of it on the part of the patient should be its own punishment. Kant, therefore, is a more sublime moralist than Bentham, and has the suffrages of all those who tell us that they love virtue for its own sake.

It is true that Bentham fulfilled his own definition of a good man: he did much good. The forty middle years of the nineteenth century in England were years of incredibly rapid progress, materially, intellectually and morally. At the beginning of the period comes the Reform Act, which made Parliament representative of the middle-class, not, as before, of the aristocracy. This Act was the most difficult of the steps towards democracy in England, and was quickly followed by other important reforms, such as the abolition of slavery in Jamaica. At the beginning of the period the penalty for petty theft was death by hanging; very soon the death penalty was confined to those who were guilty of murder or high treason. The Corn Laws, which made food so dear as to cause atrocious poverty, were abolished in 1846. Compulsory education was introduced in 1870. It is the fashion to decry the Victorians, but I wish our age had half as good a record as theirs. This, however, is beside the point. My point is that a very large proportion of the progress during those years must be attributed to the influence of Bentham. There can be no doubt that nine-tenths of the people living in England in the latter part of last century were happier than they would have been if he had never lived. So shallow was his philosophy that he would have regarded this as a vindication of his activities. We, in our more enlightened age, can see that such a view is preposterous; but it may fortify us to review the grounds for rejecting a grovelling utilitarianism such as that of Bentham.

II

We all know what we mean by a 'good' man. The ideally good man does not drink or smoke, avoids bad language, converses in the presence of men only exactly as he would if there were ladies present, attends church regularly, and holds the correct opinions on all subjects. He has a wholesome horror of wrongdoing, and realises that it is our painful duty to castigate Sin. He has a still greater horror of wrong thinking, and considers it the business of the authorities to safeguard the young against those who question the wisdom of the views generally accepted by middle-aged successful citizens. Apart from his professional duties, at which he is assiduous, he spends much time in good works: he may encourage patriotism and military training; he may promote industry, sobriety and virtue among wage-earners and their children by seeing to it that failures in these respects receive due punishment; he may be a trustee of a university and prevent an ill-judged respect for learning from allowing the employment of professors with subversive ideas. Above all, of course, his 'morals', in the narrow sense, must be irreproachable.

It may be doubted whether a 'good' man, in the above sense, does, on the average, any more good than a 'bad' man. I mean by a 'bad' man the contrary of what we have been describing. A 'bad' man is one who is known to smoke and to drink occasionally, and even to say a bad word when someone treads on his toe. His conversation is not always such as could be printed, and he sometimes spends fine Sundays out-of-doors instead of at church. Some of his opinions are subversive; for instance, he may think that if you desire peace you should prepare for peace, not for war. Towards wrongdoing he takes a scientific attitude, such as he would take towards his motorcar if it misbehaved; he argues that sermons and prison will no more cure vice than mend a broken tyre. In the matter of wrong thinking he is even more perverse. He maintains that what is called 'wrong thinking' is simply thinking, and what is called 'right thinking' is repeating words like a parrot; this gives him a sympathy with all sorts of undesirable cranks. His activities outside his working hours may consist merely in enjoyment, or, worse still, in stirring up discontent with preventable evils which do not interfere with the comfort of the men in power. And it is even possible that in the matter of 'morals' he may not conceal his lapses as carefully as a truly virtuous man would do, defending himself by the perverse contention that it is better to be honest than to pretend to set a good example. A man who fails in any or several of these respects will be thought ill of by the average respectable citizen, and will not be allowed to hold any position conferring authority, such as that of a judge, a magistrate, or a schoolmaster. Such positions are open only to 'good' men.

This whole state of affairs is more or less modern. It existed in England during the brief reign of the Puritans in the time of Cromwell, and by them it was transplanted to America. It did not reappear in force in England till after the French Revolution, when it was thought to be a good method of combating Jacobinism (i.e. what we should now call Bolshevism). The life of Wordsworth illustrates the change. In his youth he sympathised with the French Revolution, went to France, wrote good poetry, and had a natural daughter. At this period he was a 'bad' man. Then he became 'good', abandoned his daughter, adopted correct principles, and wrote bad poetry. Coleridge went through a similar change: when he was wicked he wrote *Kubla Khan*, and when he was good he wrote theology.

It is difficult to think of any instance of a poet who was 'good' at the times when he was writing good poetry. Dante was deported for subversive propaganda; Shakespeare, to judge by the Sonnets, would not have been allowed by American immigration officers to land in New York. It is of the essence of a 'good' man that he supports the Government; therefore, Milton was good during the reign of Cromwell, and bad before and after; but it was before and after that he wrote his poetry – in fact most of it was written after he had narrowly escaped hanging as a Bolshevik. Donne was virtuous after he became Dean of St Paul's, but all his poems were written before that time, and on account of them his appointment caused a scandal. Swinburne was wicked in his youth, when he wrote *Songs Before Sunrise* in praise of those who fought for freedom; he was virtuous in his old age, when he wrote savage attacks on the Boers for defending their liberty against wanton aggression. It is needless to multiply examples; enough has been said to suggest that the standards of virtue now prevalent are incompatible with the production of good poetry.

In other directions the same thing is true. We all know that Galileo and Darwin were bad men; Spinoza was thought dreadfully wicked until a hundred years after his death; Descartes went abroad for fear of persecution. Almost all the Renaissance artists were bad men. To come to humbler matters, those who object to preventable mortality are necessarily wicked. I lived in a part of London which is partly very rich, partly very poor; the infant death-rate is abnormally high, and the rich, by corruption and intimidation, control the local government. They use their power to cut down the expenditure on infant welfare and public health and to engage a medical officer at less than the standard rate on condition that he gives only half his time to the work. No one can win the respect of the important local people unless he considers that good dinners for the rich are more important than life for the children of the poor. The coresponding thing is true in every part of the world with which I am acquainted. This suggests that we may simplify our account of what constitutes a good man: a good man is one whose opinions and activities are pleasing to the holders of power.

III

It has been painful to have to dwell upon the bad men who, in the past have unfortunately achieved eminence. Let us turn to the more agreeable contemplation of the virtuous.

A typically virtuous man was George III. When Pitt wanted him to emancipate the Catholics (who at that time were not allowed to vote), he would not agree, on the ground that to do so would be contrary to his coronation oath. He righteously refused to be misled by the argument that it would do good to emancipate them; the question, for him, was not whether it would do good, but whether it was 'right' in the abstract. His interference in politics was largely responsible for the régime which caused America to claim independence; but his interference was always dictated by the most lofty motives. The same may be said of the ex-Kaiser, a deeply religious man, sincerely convinced, until his fall, that God was on his side, and (so far as I know) wholly free from personal vices. Yet it would be hard to name any man of our time who has done more to cause human misery.

Among politicians good men have their uses, the chief of which is to afford a smoke-screen behind which others can carry on their activities unsuspected. A good man will never suspect his friends of shady actions: this is part of his goodness. A good man will never be suspected by the public of using his goodness to screen villains: this is part of his utility. It is clear that this combination of qualities makes a good man extremely desirable wherever a somewhat narrow-minded public objects to the transference of public funds into the hands of the deserving rich. I am told – though far be it from me to endorse this statement – that at a not very distant period in history there was an American President who was a good man and served this purpose. In England, Whittaker Wright, at the height of his fame, surrounded himself with blameless peers, whose virtue made them incapable of understanding his arithmetic, or of knowing that they did not.

Another of the uses of good men is that any undesirables can be kept out of politics by means of scandals. Ninety-nine out of a hundred commit breaches of the moral law, but in general this fact does not become public. And when in the ninety-ninth case it becomes known in relation to any individual, the one man in the hundred who is genuinely innocent expresses genuine horror, while the other ninety-eight are compelled to follow suit for fear of being suspected. When, therefore, any man of obnoxious opinions ventures into politics, it is only necessary for those who have the preservation of our ancient institutions at heart to keep track of his private activities until they discover something which, if exposed, will ruin his political career. They then have three courses open to them: to make the facts known and cause him to disappear in a cloud of obloquy; or to compel him to retire into private life by threats of exposure; or to derive for themselves a comfortable income by means of blackmail. Of these three courses the first two protect the public, while the third protects those who protect the public. All three, therefore, are to be commended, and all three are only rendered possible through the existence of good men.

Consider, again, such a matter as venereal disease: it is known that this can be almost entirely prevented by suitable precautions taken in advance, but owing to the activities of good men this knowledge is disseminated as little as possible, and all kinds of obstacles are placed in the way of its utilisation. Consequently sin still secures its 'natural' punishment, and the children are still punished for the sins of the fathers, in accordance with Biblical precept. How dreadful it would be if this were otherwise, for, if sin were no longer punished, there might be people so abandoned as to pretend that it was no longer sin, and if the punishment did not fall also upon the innocent, it would not seem so dreadful. How grateful we ought to be, therefore, to those good men who ensure that the stern laws of retribution decreed by Nature during our days of ignorance can still be made to operate in spite of the impious knowledge rashly acquired by scientists. All right-thinking people know that a bad act is bad quite regardless of the question whether it causes any suffering or not, but since men are not all capable of being guided by the pure moral law, it is highly desirable that suffering should follow from sin in order to secure virtue. Men must be kept in ignorance of all ways of escaping the penalties which were incurred by sinful actions in pre-scientific ages. I shudder when I think how much we should all know about the preservation of mental and physical health if it were not for the protection against this dangerous knowledge which our good men so kindly provide.

Another way in which good men can be useful is by getting themselves murdered. Germany acquired the province of Shantung in China by having the good fortune to have two missionaries murdered there. The Archduke who was murdered at Sarajevo was, I believe, a good man; and how grateful we ought to be to him! If he had not died as he did, we might not have had the war, and then the world would not have been made safe for democracy, nor would militarism have been overthrown, nor should we be now enjoying military despotisms in Spain, Italy, Hungary, Bulgaria and Russia.

To speak seriously: the standards of 'goodness' which are generally recognised by public opinion are not those which are calculated to make the world a happier place. This is due to a variety of causes, of which the chief is tradition, and the next most powerful is the unjust power of dominant classes. Primitive morality seems to have developed out of the notion of taboo; that is to say, it was originally purely superstitious, and forbade certain perfectly harmless acts (such as eating out of the chief's dish) on the supposed ground that they produced disaster by magical means. In this way there came to be prohibitions, which continued to have authority over people's feelings when the supposed reasons for them were forgotten. A considerable part of current morals is still of this sort: certain kinds of conduct produce emotions of horror, quite regardless of the question whether they have bad effects or not. In many cases the conduct which inspires horror is in fact harmful; if this were not the case, the need for a revision of our moral standards would be more generally recognised. Murder, for example, can obviously not be tolerated in a civilised society; yet the origin of the prohibition of murder is purely superstitious. It was thought that the murdered man's blood (or, later, his ghost) demanded vengeance, and might punish not only the guilty man, but any one who showed him kindness. The superstitious character of the prohibition of murder is shown by the fact that it was possible to be purified from blood-guiltiness by certain ritual ceremonies, which were apparently designed, originally, to disguise the murderer so that the ghost would not recognise him. This, at least, is the theory of Sir J. G. Frazer. When we speak of repentance as 'washing out' guilt we are using a metaphor derived from the fact that long ago actual washing was used to remove blood-stains. Such notions as 'guilt' and 'sin' have an emotional background connected with this course in remote antiquity. Even in the case of murder a rational ethic will view the matter differently: it will be concerned with prevention and cure, as in the case of illness, rather than with guilt, punishment, and expiation.

Our current ethic is a curious mixture of superstition and rationalism. Murder is an ancient crime, and we view it through a mist of age-long horror. Forgery is a modern crime, and we view it rationally. We punish forgers, but we do not feel them strange beings set apart, as we do murderers. And we still think in social practice, whatever we may hold in theory, that virtue consists in not doing rather than in doing. The man who abstains from certain acts labelled 'sin' is a good man, even though he never does anything to further the welfare of others. This, of course, is not the attitude inculcated in the Gospels: 'Love thy neighbour as thyself' is a positive precept. But in all Christian communities the man who obeys this precept is persecuted, suffering at least poverty, usually imprisonment, and sometimes death. The world is full of injustice, and those who profit by injustice are in a position to administer rewards and punishments. The rewards go to those who invent ingenious justifications for inequality, the punishments to those who try to remedy it. I do not know of any country where a man who has a genuine love for his neighbour can long avoid obloquy. In Paris, just before the outbreak of the war, Jean Jaurès, the best citizen of France, was murdered; the murderer was acquitted, on the ground that he had performed a public service. This case was peculiarly dramatic, but the same sort of thing happens everywhere.

Those who defend traditional morality will sometimes admit that it is not perfect, but contend that any criticism will make all morality crumble. This will not be the case if the criticism is based upon something positive and constructive, but only if it is conducted with a view to nothing more than momentary pleasure. To return to Bentham: he advocated, as the basis of morals, 'the greatest happiness of the greatest number'. A man who acts upon this principle will have a much more arduous life than a man who merely obeys conventional precepts. He will necessarily make himself the champion of the oppressed, and so incur the enmity of the great. He will proclaim facts which the powers that be wish to conceal; he will deny falsehoods designed to alienate sympathy from those who need it. Such a mode of life does not lead to a collapse of genuine morality. Official morality has always been oppressive and negative: it has said 'thou shalt not', and has not troubled to investigate the effect of activities not forbidden by the code. Against this kind of morality all the great mystics and religious teachers have protested in vain: their followers ignored their most explicit pronouncements. It seems unlikely, therefore, that any large-scale improvements will come through their methods.

More is to be hoped, I think, from the progress of reason and science. Gradually men will come to realise that a world whose institutions are based upon hatred and injustice is not the one most likely to produce happiness. The late war taught this lesson to a few, and would have taught it to many more if it had ended in a draw. We need a morality based upon love of life, upon pleasure in growth and positive achievement, not upon repression and prohibition. A man should be regarded as 'good' if he is happy, expansive, generous and glad when others are happy; if so, a few peccadilloes should be regarded as of little importance. But a man who acquires a fortune by cruelty and exploitation should be regarded as at present we regard what is called an 'immoral' man; and he should be so regarded even if he goes to church regularly and gives a portion of his ill-gotten gains to public objects. To bring this about, it is only necessary to instil a rational attitude towards ethical questions, instead of the mixture of superstition and oppression which still passes muster as 'virtue' among important personages. The power of reason is thought small in these days, but I remain an unrepentant rationalist. Reason may be a small force, but it is constant, and works always in one direction, while the forces of unreason destroy one another in futile strife. Therefore every orgy of unreason in the end strengthens the friends of reason, and shows afresh that they are the only true friends of humanity.

Chapter 10

breaking out again / revival

The Recrudescence of Puritanism

During the war, the holders of power in all countries found it necessary to bribe the populations into co-operation by unusual concessions. Wage-earners were allowed a living wage, Hindoos were told that they were men and brothers, women were given the vote, and young people were allowed to enjoy those innocent pleasures of which the old, in the name of morality, always wish to rob them. The war being won, the victors set to work to deprive their tools of the advantages temporarily conceded. Wage-earners were worsted by the coal strikes in 1921 and 1926; Hindoos have been put in their place by various decisions; women, though they could not be deprived of the vote, have been ousted from posts when they married, in spite of an Act of Parliament saying that this should not be done. All these issues are 'political' – that is to say, there are organised bodies of voters representing the interests of the classes concerned in England, and organised bodies of resisters in India. But no organised body represents the point of view of those who believe that a man or woman ought to be free in regard to enjoyments which do not damage other people, so that the Puritans have met with no serious opposition, and their tyranny has not been regarded as raising a political issue.

We may define a Puritan as a man who holds that certain kinds of acts, even if they have no visible bad effects upon others than the agent, are inherently sinful, and, being sinful, ought to be prevented by whatever means is most effectual – the criminal law if possible, and, if not that, then public opinion backed by economic pressure. This view is of respectable antiquity; indeed, it was probably responsible for the origin of criminal law. But originally it was reconciled with a utilitarian basis of legislation by the belief that certain crimes roused the anger of the gods against communities which tolerated them, and were therefore socially harmful.

This point of view is embodied in the story of Sodom and Gomorrah. Those who believe this story can justify, on utilitarian grounds, the existing laws against the crimes which led to the destruction of those cities. But nowadays even Puritans seldom adopt this point of view. Not even the Bishop of London has suggested that the earthquake in Tokyo was due to any peculiar wickedness of its inhabitants. The laws in question can, therefore, only be justified by the theory of vindictive punishment, which holds that certain sins, though they may not injure anyone except the sinner, are so heinous as to make it our duty to inflict pain upon the delinquent. This point of view, under the influence of Benthamism, lost its hold during the nineteenth century. But in recent years, with the general decay of Liberalism, it has regained lost ground, and has begun to threaten a new tyranny as oppressive as any in the Middle Ages.

It is from America that the new movement derives most of its force; it is one consequence of the fact that America was the sole victor in the war. The career of Puritanism has been curious. It held brief power in England in the seventeenth century, but so disgusted the mass of ordinary citizens that they have never again allowed it to control the Government. The Puritans, persecuted in England, colonised New England, and subsequently the Middle West. The American Civil War was a continuation of the English Civil War, the Southern States having been mainly colonised by opponents of the Puritans. But unlike the English Civil War, it led to a permanent victory of the Puritan Party. The result is that the greatest Power in the world is controlled by men who inherit the outlook of Cromwell's Ironsides.

It would be unfair to point out the drawbacks of Puritanism without acknowledging its services to mankind. In England, in the seventeenth century and until modern times, it has stood for democracy against royal and aristocratic tyranny. In America, it stood for emancipation of the slaves, and did much to make America the champion of democracy throughout the world. These are great services to mankind, but they belong to the past. The problem of the present is not so much political democracy as the combination of order with liberty for minorities. This problem requires a different outlook from that of Puritanism; it requires tolerance and breadth of sympathy rather than moral fervour. Breadth of sympathy has never been a strong point with the Puritans.

I will not say anything about the most noteworthy victory of Puritanism, namely, Prohibition in America. In any case, opponents of Prohibition cannot well make their opposition a matter of principle, since most of them would favour the prohibition of cocaine, which raises exactly the same questions of principle.

The practical objection to Puritanism, as to every form of fanaticism, is that it singles out certain evils as so much worse than others that they must be suppressed at all costs. The fanatic fails to recognise that the suppression of a real evil, if carried out too drastically, produces other evils which are even greater. We may illustrate by the law against obscene publications. No one denies that pleasure in obscenity is base, or that those who minister to it do harm. But when the law steps in to suppress it, much that is highly desirable is suppressed at the same time. A few years ago, certain pictures by an eminent Dutch artist were sent through the post to an English purchaser. The Post Office officials, after enjoying a thorough inspection of them, concluded that they were obscene. (Appreciation of artistic merit is not expected of Civil Servants.) They therefore destroyed them, and the purchaser had no redress. The law gives power to the Post Office to destroy anything sent through the post that the officials consider obscene, and from their decision there is no appeal.

A more important example of the evils resulting from Puritan legislation arises in connection with birth control. It is obvious that 'obscenity' is not a term capable of exact legal definition; in the practice of the Courts, it means 'anything that shocks the magistrate'. Now an average magistrate is not shocked by information about birth control if it is given in an expensive book which uses long words and roundabout phrases, but is shocked if it is given in a cheap pamphlet using plain language that uneducated people can understand. Consequently it is at present illegal in England to give information on birth control to wage-earners, though it is legal to give it to educated people. Yet it is wage-earners above all to whom the information is important. It should be noted that the law takes no account whatever of the purpose of a publication, except in a few recognised cases such as medical textbooks. The sole question to be considered is: If this publication fell into the hands of a nasty-minded boy, could it give him pleasure? If so, it must be destroyed, whatever the social importance of the information it contains. The harm done by the enforced ignorance which results is incalculable. Destitution, chronic illness among women, the birth of diseased children, over-population and war are regarded by our Puritan lawgivers as smaller evils than the hypothetical pleasure of a few foolish boys.

The law as it exists is thought to be not sufficiently drastic. Under the auspices of the League of Nations, an International Conference on Obscene Publications, as reported in *The Times* of September 17, 1923, recommended a tightening-up of the law in the United States and in all the countries belonging to the League of Nations. The British delegate was apparently the most zealous in this good work.

Another matter which has been made the basis for far-reaching legislation is the white-slave traffic. The real evil here is very grave, and is quite a proper matter for the criminal law. The real evil is that ignorant young women are enticed by false promises into a condition of semi-slavery in which their health is exposed to the gravest dangers. It is essentially a Labour question, to be dealt with on the lines of the Factory Acts and the Truck Acts. But it has been made the excuse for gross interference with personal liberty in cases where the peculiar evils of the white-slave traffic are entirely absent. Some years ago a case was reported in the English papers in which a man had fallen in love with a prostitute and married her. After they had lived together happily for some time, she decided to go back to her old profession. There was no evidence that he suggested her doing so, or in any way approved of her action, but he did not at once quarrel with her and turn her out of doors. For this crime he was flogged and thrown into prison. He suffered this punishment under a law which was then recent, and which is still on the statute-book.

In America, under a similar law, though it is not illegal to keep a mistress, it is illegal to travel with her from one State to another; a New Yorker may take his mistress to Brooklyn but not to Jersey City. The difference of moral turpitude between these two actions is not obvious to the plain man.

On this matter, also, the League of Nations is endeavouring to secure more severe legislation. Some time ago, the Canadian delegate on the League of Nations Commission suggested that no woman, however old, should be allowed to travel on a steamer unless accompanied by her husband or by one of her parents. This proposal was not adopted, but it illustrates the direction in which we are moving. It is, of course, obvious that such measures turn all women into 'white slaves'; women cannot have any freedom without a risk that some will use it for purposes of 'immorality'. The only logical goal of these reformers is the purdah.

There is another more general argument against the Puritan outlook. Human nature being what it is, people will insist upon getting some pleasure out of life. For rough practical purposes, pleasures may be divided into those that have their primary basis in the senses, and those that are mainly of the mind. The traditional moralist praises the latter at the expense of the former; or rather, he tolerates the latter because he does not recognise them as pleasures. His classification is, of course, not scientifically defensible, and in many cases he is himself in doubt. Do the pleasures of art belong to the senses or to the mind? If he is really stern, he will condemn art *in toto*, like Plato and the Fathers: if he is more or less latitudinarian, he will tolerate art if it has a 'spiritual purpose', which generally means that it is bad art. This is Tolstoy's view. Marriage is another difficult case. The stricter moralists regard it as regrettable; the less strict praise it on the ground that it is generally unpleasant, especially when they succeed in making it indissoluble.

This, however, is not my point. My point is that pleasures which remain possible after the Puritan has done his utmost are more harmful than those that he condemns. Next to enjoying ourselves, the next greatest pleasure consists in preventing others from enjoying themselves, or, more generally, in the acquisition of power. Consequently those who live under the dominion of Puritanism become exceedingly desirous of power. Now love of power does far more harm than love of drink or any of the other vices against which Puritans protest. Of course, in virtuous people love of power camouflages itself as love of doing good, but this makes very little difference to its social effects. It merely means that we punish our victims for being wicked, instead of for being our enemies. In either case, tyranny and war result. Moral indignation is one of the most harmful forces in the modern world, the more so as it can always be diverted to sinister uses by those who control propaganda.

Economic and political organisation has inevitably increased with the growth of industrialism, and is bound to increase still further unless industrialism collapses. The earth becomes more crowded, and our dependence upon our neighbours becomes more intimate. In these circumstances life cannot remain tolerable unless we learn to let each other alone in all matters that are not of immediate and obvious concern to the community. We must learn to respect each other's privacy, and not to impose our moral standards upon each other. The Puritan imagines that his moral standard is *the* moral standard; he does not realise that other ages and other countries, and even other groups in his own country, have moral standards different from his, to which they have as good a right as he has to his. Unfortunately, the love of power which is the natural outcome of Puritan self-denial makes the Puritan more executive than other people, and makes it difficult for others to resist him. Let us hope that a broader education and a wider knowledge of mankind may gradually weaken the ardour of our too virtuous masters.

Chapter 11

The Need for Political Scepticism [1]

One of the peculiarities of the English-speaking world is its immense interest and belief in political parties. A very large percentage of English-speaking people really believe that the ills from which they suffer would be cured if a certain political party were in power. That is a reason for the swing of the pendulum. A man votes for one party and remains miserable; he concludes that it was the other party that was to bring the millennium. By the time he is disenchanted with all parties, he is an old man on the verge of death; his sons retain the belief of his youth, and the see-saw goes on.

I want to suggest that, if we are to do any good in politics, we must view political questions in quite a different way. A party which is to obtain power must, in a democracy, make an appeal to which the majority of the nation responds. For reasons which will appear in the course of the argument, an appeal which is widely successful, with the existing democracy, can hardly fail to be harmful. Therefore no important political party is likely to have a useful programme, and if useful measures are to be passed, it must be by means of some other machinery than party government. How to combine any such machinery with democracy is one of the most urgent problems of our time.

There are at present two very different kinds of specialists in political questions. On the one hand there are the practical politicians of all parties; on the other hand there are the experts, mainly civil servants, but also economists, financiers, scientific medical men, etc. Each of these two classes has a special kind of skill. The skill of the politician consists in guessing what people can be brought to *think* advantageous to themselves; the skill of

[1] Presidential Address to the Students' Union of the London School of Economics and Political Science, October 10th, 1923.

the expert consists in calculating what really *is* advantageous, provided people can be brought to think so. (The proviso is essential, because measures which arouse serious resentment are seldom advantageous, whatever merits they may have otherwise.) The power of the politician, in a democracy, depends upon his adopting the opinions which *seem* right to the average man. It is useless to urge that politicians ought to be high-minded enough to advocate what enlightened opinion considers good, because if they do they are swept aside for others. Moreover, the intuitive skill that they require in forecasting opinion does not imply any skill whatever in forming their own opinions, so that many of the ablest (from a party-political point of view) will be in a position to advocate, quite honestly, measures which the majority think good, but which experts know to be bad. There is therefore no point in moral exhortations to politicians to be disinterested, except in the crude sense of not taking bribes.

Wherever party politics exist, the appeal of a politician is primarily to a section, while his opponents appeal to an opposite section. His success depends upon turning his section into a majority. A measure which appeals to all sections equally will presumably be common ground between the parties, and will therefore be useless to the party politician. Consequently he concentrates attention upon those measures which are disliked by the section which forms the nucleus of his opponents' supporters. Moreover, a measure, however admirable, is useless to the politician unless he can give reasons for it which will appear convincing to the average man when set forth in a platform speech. We have thus two conditions which must be fulfilled by the measures on which party politicians lay stress: (1) they must seem to favour a section of the nation; (2) the arguments for them must be of the utmost simplicity. Of course this does not apply to a time of war, because then the party conflict is suspended in favour of conflict with the external enemy. In war, the arts of the politician are expended on neutrals, who correspond to the doubtful voter in ordinary politics. The late war showed that, as we should have expected, democracy affords an admirable training for the business of appealing to neutrals. That was one of the main reasons why democracy won the war. It is true it lost the peace; but that is another question.

The special skill of the politician consists in knowing what passions can be most easily aroused, and how to prevent them, when aroused, from being harmful to himself and his associates. There is a Gresham's law in politics as in currency; a man who aims at nobler ends than these will be driven out except in those rare moments (chiefly revolutions) when idealism finds itself in alliance with some powerful movement of selfish passion. Moreover, since politicians are divided into rival groups, they aim at similarly dividing the nation, unless they have the good fortune to unite it in war against some other nation. They live by 'sound and fury, signifying nothing'. They cannot pay attention to anything difficult to explain, or to anything not involving division (either between nations or within the nation), or to anything that would diminish the power of politicians as a class.

The expert is a curiously different type. As a rule, he is a man who does not aim at political power. His natural reaction to a political problem is to inquire what would be beneficial rather than what would be popular. In certain directions, he has exceptional technical knowledge. If he is a civil servant or the head of a big business, he has considerable experience of individual men, and may be a shrewd judge as to how they will act. All these are favourable circumstances, which entitle his opinion on his speciality to considerable respect.

He has, however, as a rule, certain correlative defects. His knowledge being specialised, he probably overestimates the importance of his department. If you went successively to a scientific dentist, a scientific oculist, a heart specialist, a lung specialist, a nerve specialist, and so on, they would each give you admirable advice as to how to prevent their particular kind of ailment. If you followed the advice of all, you would find your whole twenty-four hours consumed in preserving your health, and no time left to make any use of your health. The same sort of thing may easily happen with political experts; if all are attended to, there will be no time for the nation to live its ordinary life.

A second defect of the able civil servant results from his having to use the method of persuasion behind the scenes. He will either greatly overestimate the possibility of persuading people to be reasonable, or he will prefer hole-and-corner methods, by which politicians are induced to pass crucial measures without knowing what they are doing. As a rule, he will make the former mistake when he is young and the latter when he is middle-aged.

A third defect of the expert, if regarded as one who is to have executive power, is that he is no judge of popular passions. He usually understands a committee very well, but he seldom understands a mob. Having discovered some measure which all well-informed persons of good will at once see to be desirable, he does not realise that, if it is publicly advocated, certain powerful people who think it will damage themselves can stir up popular feeling to the point where any advocate of the measure in question will be lynched. In America, the magnates, it is said, set detectives on to any man they dislike, and presently, if he is not exceptionally astute, manoeuvre him into a compromising situation. He must then either change his politics or be denounced throughout the Press as an immoral man. In England, these methods are not yet so well developed, but they probably will be before long. Even where there is nothing sinister, popular passions are often such as to astonish the unwary. Everybody wishes the Government to cut down expenditure in general, but any particular economy is always unpopular, because it throws individuals out of work, and they win sympathy. In China, in the eleventh century, there was a civil servant, Wang An Shih, who, having converted the Emperor, set to work to introduce Socialism. In a rash moment, however, he offended the literati (the Northcliffe Press of that time), was hurled from power, and has been held up to obloquy by every subsequent Chinese historian until modern times.

A fourth defect is connected with this, namely, that experts are apt to undervalue the importance of consent to administrative measures, and to ignore the difficulty of administering an unpopular law. Medical men could, if they had power, devise means which would stamp out infectious diseases, provided their laws were obeyed; but if their laws went much ahead of public opinion, they would be evaded. The case of administration during the war was due to the fact that people would submit to a great deal in order to win the war, whereas ordinary peace legislation has no object making such a strong appeal.

Hardly any expert allows enough for sheer laziness and indifference. We take some trouble to avoid dangers which are obvious, but very little to avoid those only visible to the expert. We think we like money, and daylight saving saves us many millions a year; yet we never adopted it until we were driven to it as a war-measure. We love our habits more than our income, often more than our life. This seems incredible to a person who has reflected upon the harmfulness of some of our habits.

Probably most experts do not realise that, if they had executive power, their impulses toward tyranny would develop, and they would cease to be the amiable and high-minded men they are at present. Very few people are able to discount the effect of circumstances upon their own characters.

For all these reasons, we cannot escape from the evils of our present politicians by simply handing over the power to civil servants. Nevertheless it seems imperative, in our increasingly complex society, that experts should acquire more influence than they have at present. There is at present a violent conflict between instinctive passions and industrial needs. Our environment, both human and material, has been suddenly changed by industrialism. Our instincts have presumably not changed, and almost nothing has been done to adapt our habits of thought to the altered circumstances. Unwise people who keep beavers in their libraries find that, when wet weather is coming, the beavers build dams out of books, because they used to live on the banks of streams. We are almost equally ill-adapted to our new surroundings. Our education still teaches us to admire the qualities that were biologically useful in the Homeric age, regardless of the fact that they are now harmful and ridiculous. The instinctive appeal of every successful political movement is to envy, rivalry or hate, never to the need for co-operation. This is inherent in our present political methods, and in conformity with pre-industrial habits. Only a deliberate effort can change men's habits of thought in this respect.

It is a natural propensity to attribute misfortune to someone's malignity. When prices rise, it is due to the profiteer; when wages fall, it is due to the capitalist. Why the capitalist is ineffective when wages rise, and the profiteer when prices fall, the man in the street does not inquire. Nor does he notice that wages and prices rise and fall together. If he is a capitalist, he wants wages to fall and prices to rise; if he is a wage earner, he wants the opposite. When a currency expert tries to explain that profiteers and trade unions and ordinary employers have very little to do with the matter, he irritates everybody, like the man who threw doubt on German atrocities. We do not like to be robbed of an enemy; we want someone to hate when we suffer. It is so depressing to think that we suffer because we are fools; yet, taking mankind in the mass, that is the truth. For this reason, no political party can acquire any driving force except through hatred; it must hold up someone to obloquy. If so-and-so's wickedness is the sole cause of our misery, let us punish so-and-so and we shall be happy. The supreme example of this kind of political thought was the Treaty of Versailles. Yet most people are only seeking some new scapegoat to replace the Germans.

I will illustrate the point by contrasting two books advocating international Socialism, Marx's *Capital* and Salter's *Allied Shipping Control*. (No doubt Sir Arther Salter does not call himself an international socialist, but he is one none the less.) We may take these two books as representing the politician's and the civil servant's methods, respectively, of advocating economic change. Marx's object was to create a political party which should ultimately overwhelm all others; Salter's object is to influence administrators within the existing system, and to modify public opinion by arguments based upon the general advantage. Marx proves conclusively that under capitalism wage-earners have suffered terrible privations. He does not prove, and does not attempt to prove, that they will suffer less under Communism; that is an assumption implicit in his style and in the ordering of his chapters. Any reader who starts with a proletarian class bias will find himself sharing this assumption as he reads, and will never notice that it is not proved. Again: Marx emphatically repudiates ethical considerations as having nothing to do with social development, which is supposed to proceed by inexorable economic laws, just as in Ricardo and Malthus. But Ricardo and Malthus thought that the inexorable laws inexorably brought happiness to their class along with misery to wage-earners; while Marx, like Tertullian, had an apocalyptic vision of a future in which his class would enjoy the circuses while the bourgeois would lie howling. Although Marx professed to regard men as neither good nor bad, but merely embodiments of economic forces, he did in fact represent the bourgeois as wicked, and set to work to stimulate a fiery hatred of him in the wage-earner. Marx's *Capital* is in essence, like the Bryce Report, a collection of atrocity stories designed to stimulate martial ardour against the enemy.[1] Very naturally, it

[1] The theoretical part of *Capital* is analogous to our talk about a 'war to end war', a 'war for small nations', a 'war for democracy', etc. Its sole

also stimulates the martial ardour of the enemy. It thus brings about the class-war which it prophesies. It is through the stimulation of hatred that Marx has proved such a tremendous political force, and through the fact that he has successfully represented capitalists as objects of moral abhorrence.

In Salter's *Allied Shipping Control* we find a diametrically opposite spirit. Salter has the advantage, which Marx had not, of having been for some time concerned in administering a system of international Socialism. This system was brought about, not by the desire to kill capitalists, but by the desire to kill Germans. As, however, the Germans were irrelevant to economic issues, they are in the background in Salter's book. The economic problem was exactly the same as if the soldiers and munition-workers and those who supplied the raw materials of munitions had been kept in idleness and the remainder of the population had had to do all the work. Or, alternatively, as if it had been suddenly decreed that everybody was to do only half as much work as hitherto. War experience has given us a *technical* solution of this problem, but not a *psychological* solution, because it has not shown how to provide a stimulus to co-operation in peace-time as powerful as hatred and fear of the Germans during the years of war.

Salter says (p. 19):

'There is probably no task at this moment which more deserves the attention of professional economists who will approach the problem in a purely scientific spirit, without bias either for or against the principle of State control, than an investigation of the actual results of the war period. The *prima facie* facts with which they would start are indeed so striking as to constitute at least a challenge to the normal economic system. It is true that several factors contributed to the results. ... An unbiased professional inquiry would assign full weight to these and other factors, but would probably find much still to the credit of the new methods of organisation. The success of these methods under the conditions of the war is indeed beyond reasonable dispute. At a moderate estimate, and allowing for the production of persons who were idle before the war, between half and two-thirds of the productive

---

purpose is to make the reader feel that the hatred stirred up in him is righteous indignation, and may be indulged with benefit to mankind.

capacity of the country was withdrawn into combatant or other war service. And yet throughout the War Great Britain sustained the whole of her military effort and maintained civilian population at a standard of life which was never intolerably low, and for some periods and for some classes was perhaps as comfortable as in time of peace. She did this without, on balance, drawing any aid from other countries. She imported, on borrowed money, less from America than she supplied, on loaned money, to her Allies. She therefore maintained the whole of the current consumption both of her war effort and her civilian population with a mere remnant of her productive power by means of current production.'

Discussing the ordinary commercial system of peace-time, he says:

'It was thus of the essence of the peace economic system that it was under no deliberate direction and control. By the exacting criterion of war conditions, however, this system proved to be, at least for those conditions, seriously inadequate and defective. By the new standards it was blind and it was wasteful. It produced too little, it produced the wrong things, and it distributed them to the wrong people.' (p. 17).

The system which was gradually built up under the stress of war became, in 1918, in all essentials a complete international Socialism. The Allied Governments jointly were the sole buyer of food and raw material, and the sole judge as to what should be imported, not only into their own countries, but even into those of European neutrals. They controlled production absolutely, because they controlled raw material, and could ration factories as they chose. As regards food they even controlled retail distribution. They fixed prices as well as quantities. Their power was exercised mainly through the Allied Maritime Transport Council, which, in the end, controlled nearly all the world's available shipping, and was consequently able to dictate the conditions of import and export. The system was thus, in all essentials, one of international Socialism, applied primarily to foreign trade, the very matter which causes the greatest difficulties to political socialists.

The odd thing about this system is that it was introduced without antagonising the capitalists. It was a necessary feature of war-time politics that at all costs no important section of the population must be antagonised. For instance, at the time of greatest stringency in the shipping position, it was argued that munitions must be cut down rather than food, for fear of discontent in the civilian population. To have alienated the capitalists would have been very dangerous, and in fact the whole transformation was carried out without serious friction. The attitude was not: Such-and-such classes of men are wicked and must be punished. The attitude was: The peace-time system was inefficient, and a new system must be established with a minimum of hardship to all concerned. Under the stress of national danger, consent to measures which the Government considered necessary was not so difficult to obtain as it would be at ordinary times. But even at ordinary times consent would be less difficult if measures were presented from an administrative point of view rather than from that of class-antagonism.

It would appear from the administrative experience of the war that most of the advantages hoped from Socialism can be obtained by Government control of raw materials, foreign trade, and banking. This point of view has been developed by Lloyd's valuable book of *Stabilization*.[1] It may be taken as a definite advance in the scientific analysis of the problem, which we owe to the experimentation forced upon civil servants by the war.

One of the most interesting things, from a practical point of view, in Sir Arthur Salter's book is his analysis of the methods of international co-operation which was found to work best in practice. It was not the custom for each country separately to consider each question, and then employ diplomatic representatives to secure as much as possible in bargaining with other Powers. The plan adopted was for each question to have its separate international committee of experts, so that the conflicts were not between nations, but between commodities. The wheat commission would fight the coal commission, and so on; but the recommendations of each were the result of deliberation between expert representatives of the different Allies. The position, in fact, was almost one of international syndicalism, except for the paramount authority of the Supreme War Council. The moral is that any successful internationalism must organise separate functions

[1] George Allen & Unwin, 1923.

internationally, and not merely have one supreme international body to adjust the claims of conflicting purely national bodies.

Any person reading Salter's book can see at once that such an international government as existed among the Allies during the war would increase the material, mental and moral welfare of almost the whole population of the globe, if it could be established universally in time of peace. It would not injure business men; indeed, they could easily be promised in perpetuity, as a pension, their average profits for the last three years. It would prevent unemployment, fear of war, destitution, shortage and over-production. The argument and the method are set forth in Mr Lloyd's book. Yet, in spite of these obvious and universal advantages, the prospect of anything of the sort is, if possible, even more remote than the establishment of universal revolutionary Socialism. The difficulty of revolutionary Socialism is that it rouses too much opposition; the difficulty of the civil servant's Socialism is that it wins too little support. Opposition to a political measure is roused by the fear that oneself will be damaged; support is won by the hope (usually subconscious) that one's enemies will be damaged. Therefore a policy that injures no one wins no support, and a policy that wins much support also rouses fierce opposition.

Industrialism has created a new necessity for world-wide co-operation and a new facility for injuring each other by hostility. But the only kind of appeal that wins any instinctive response in party politics is an appeal to hostile feeling; the men who perceive the need of co-operation are powerless. Until education has been directed for a generation into new channels, and the Press has abandoned incitements to hatred, only harmful policies have any chance of being adopted in practice by our present political methods. But there is no obvious means of altering education and the Press until our political system is altered. From this dilemma there is no issue by means of ordinary action, at any rate for a long time to come. The best that can be hoped, it seems to me, is that we should, as many of us as possible, become political sceptics, rigidly abstaining from belief in the various attractive party programmes that are put before us from time to time. Many quite sensible people, from Mr H. G. Wells downward, believed that the late war was a war to end war. They are now disillusioned. Many quite sensible people believe that the Marxian class war will be a war to end war. If it ever comes, they too will be disillusioned

– if any of them survive. A well-intentioned person who believes in any strong political movement is merely helping to prolong that organised strife which is destroying our civilisation. Of course I do not lay this down as an absolute rule: we must be sceptical even of our scepticism. But if a political party has a policy (as most have) which must do much harm on the way to some ultimate good, the call for scepticism is very great, in view of the doubtfulness of all political calculations. We may fairly suspect that, from a psycho-analytic point of view, the harm to be done by the way is what makes the policy really attractive, and the ultimate good is of the nature of a 'rationalising'.

Widespread political scepticism is possible; psychologically, it means concentrating our enmity upon politicians, instead of nations or social classes. Since enmity cannot be effective except by the help of politicians, an enmity of which they are the objects may be psychologically satisfying, but cannot be socially harmful. I suggest it as fulfilling the conditions for William James's desideratum, a 'moral equivalent for war'. True, it would leave politics to obvious scoundrels (i.e. persons whom you and I dislike), but that might be a gain. I read in *The Freeman* of September 26, 1923, a story which may illustrate the usefulness of political scoundrelism. A certain Englishman, having made friends with a Japanese Elder Statesman, asked him why Chinese merchants were honest while those of Japan were not. 'Some time ago,' he replied, 'a period of particularly brilliant corruption set in in Chinese politics, and as far as the Courts were concerned, justice became a mockery. Hence, in order to save the processes of trade from complete chaos and stagnation, the Chinese merchant was compelled to adopt the strictest ethical standards; and since that time his word has been as good as his bond. In Japan, however, the merchant has been under no such compulsion, for we have probably the finest code of legal justice in the world. Hence when you do business with a Japanese, you must take 'your chances.' This story shows that dishonest politicians may do less harm than honest ones.

The conception of an 'honest' politician is not altogether a simple one. The most tolerant definition is: one whose political actions are not dictated by a desire to increase his own income. In this sense, Mr Lloyd George is honest. The next stage would be the man whose political actions are not dictated by desire to secure or preserve his own power any more than by pecuniary motives. In this sense, Lord Grey is an honest politician. The last and most stringent sense is: one who, in his public actions, is not only disinterested, but does not fall very far below the standard of veracity and honour which is taken for granted between acquaintance. In this sense, the late Lord Morley was an honest politician; at least, he was honest always, and a politician until his honesty drove him out of politics. But even a politician who is honest in the highest sense may be very harmful; one may take George III as an illustration. Stupidity and unconscious bias often work more damage than venality. Moreover, an honest politician will not be tolerated by a democracy unless he is very stupid, like the late Duke of Devonshire; because only a very stupid man can honestly share the prejudices of more than half the nation. Therefore any man who is both able and public-spirited must be a hypocrite if he is to succeed in politics; but the hypocrisy will in time destroy his public spirit.

One obvious palliative of the evils of democracy in its present form would be to encourage much more publicity and initiative on the part of civil servants. They ought to have the right, and, on occasion, the duty, to frame Bills in their own names, and set forth publicly the arguments in their favour. Finance and Labour already have international conferences, but they ought to extend this method enormously, and cause an international secretariat to be perpetually considering measures to be simultaneously advocated in different countries. The agricultural interests of the world ought to meet for direct negotiations and adoption of a common policy. And so on. It is neither possible nor desirable to dispense with democratic parliaments, because measures which are to succeed must, after due discussion and the dissemination of considered expert opinions, be such as to commend themselves to the ordinary citizen. But at present, in most matters, the ordinary citizen does not know the considered opinion of experts, and little machinery exists for arriving at their collective or majority opinion. In particular, civil servants are debarred from public advocacy of their views, except in exceptional cases and by non-political methods. If measures were framed by experts after international deliberation, they would cut across party lines, and would be found to involve far less division of opinion than is now taken for granted. I believe, for example, that international finance and international labour, if they could overcome their mutual distrust, could at this moment agree on a programme which would take the national Parliaments several years to carry out, and would improve the world immeasurably. In unison, they would be difficult to resist.

The common interests of mankind are numerous and weighty, but our existing political machinery obscures them through the scramble for power between different nations and different parties. A different machinery, requiring no legal or constitutional changes, and not very difficult to create, would undermine the strength of national and party passion, and focus attention upon measures beneficial to all rather than upon those damaging to enemies. I suggest that it is along these lines, rather than by party government at home and foreign-office diplomacy abroad, that an issue is to be found from the present peril to civilisation. Knowledge exists, and good will exists; but both remain impotent until they possess the proper organs for making themselves heard.

Chapter 12

Free Thought and Official Propaganda[1]

Moncure Conway, in whose honour we are assembled today, devoted his life to two great objects: freedom of thought, and freedom of the individual. In regard to both these objects, something has been gained since his time, but something also has been lost. New dangers, somewhat different in form from those of past ages, threaten both kinds of freedom, and unless a vigorous and vigilant public opinion can be aroused in defence of them, there will be much less of both a hundred years hence than there is now. My purpose in this essay is to emphasise the new dangers and to consider how they can be met.

Let us begin by trying to be clear as to what we mean by 'free thought'. This expression has two senses. In its narrower sense it means thought which does not accept the dogmas of traditional religion. In this sense a man is a 'free thinker' if he is not a Christian or a Mussulman or a Buddhist or a Shintoist or a member of any of the other bodies of men who accept some inherited orthodoxy. In Christian countries a man is called a 'free thinker' if he does not decidedly believe in God, though this would not suffice to make a man a 'free thinker' in a Buddhist country.

I do not wish to minimise the importance of free thought in this sense. I am myself a dissenter from all known religions, and I hope that every kind of religious belief will die out. I do not believe that, on the balance, religious belief has been a force for good. Although I am prepared to admit that in certain times and places it has had some good effects, I regard it as belonging to the infancy of human reason, and to a stage of development which we are now outgrowing.

But there is also a wider sense of 'free thought', which I regard as of still greater importance. Indeed, the harm done by tradi-

[1] Moncure Conway Lecture for 1922.

tional religions seems chiefly traceable to the fact that they have prevented free thought in this wider sense. The wider sense is not so easy to define as the narrower, and it will be well to spend some little time in trying to arrive at its essence.

When we speak of anything as 'free', our meaning is not definite unless we can say what it is free from. Whatever or whoever is 'free' is not subject to some external compulsion, and to be precise we ought to say what this kind of compulsion is. Thus thought is 'free' when it is free from certain kinds of outward control which are often present. Some of these kinds of control which must be absent if thought is to be 'free' are obvious, but others are more subtle and elusive.

To begin with the most obvious: thought is not 'free' when legal penalties are incurred by the holding or not holding of certain opinions, or by giving expression to one's belief or lack of belief on certain matters. Very few countries in the world have as yet even this elementary kind of freedom. In England, under the blasphemy laws, it is illegal to express disbelief in the Christian religion, though in practice the law is not set in motion against the well-to-do.[1] It is also illegal to teach what Christ taught on the subject of non-resistance. Therefore whoever wishes to avoid becoming a criminal must profess to agree with Christ's teaching, but must avoid saying what that teaching was. In America, no one can enter the country without first solemnly declaring that he disbelieves in anarchism and polygamy; and once inside, he must also disbelieve in Communism. In Japan, it is illegal to express disbelief in the divinity of the Mikado. It will thus be seen that a voyage round the world is a perilous adventure. A Mahometan, a Tolstoyan, a Bolshevik, or a Christian cannot undertake it without at some point becoming a criminal, or holding his tongue about what he considers important truths. This of course only applies to steerage passengers; saloon passengers are allowed to believe whatever they please, provided they avoid offensive obtrusiveness.

It is clear that the most elementary condition, if thought is to be free, is the absence of legal penalties for the expression of opinions. No great country has yet reached to this level, although most of them think they have. The opinions which are still persecuted strike the majority as so monstrous and immoral that the

[1] In New Zealand there is no such limitation. A publisher has been convicted of blasphemy for publishing Sassoon's poems.

general principle of toleration cannot be held to apply to them. But this is exactly the same view as that which made possible the tortures of the Inquisition. There was a time when Protestantism seemed as wicked as Bolshevism seems now. Please do not infer from this remark that I am either a Prostestant or a Bolshevik.

Legal penalties are, however, in the modern world, the least of the obstacles to freedom of thought. The two great obstacles are economic penalties and distortion of evidence. It is clear that thought is not free if the profession of certain opinions makes it impossible to earn a living. It is clear also that thought is not free if all the arguments on one side of a controversy are perpetually presented as attractively as possible, while the arguments on the other side can only be discovered by diligent search. Both these obstacles exist in every large country known to me, except China, which is (or was) the last refuge of freedom. It is these obstacles with which I shall be concerned – their present magnitude, the likelihood of their increase, and the possibility of their diminution.

We may say that thought is free when it is exposed to free competition among beliefs, i.e. when all beliefs are able to state their case, and no legal or pecuniary advantages or disadvantages attach to beliefs. This is an ideal which, for various reasons, can never be fully attained. But it is possible to approach very much nearer to it than we do at present.

Three incidents in my own life will serve to show how, in modern England, the scales are weighted in favour of Christianity. My reason for mentioning them is that many people do not at all realise the disadvantages to which avowed agnosticism still exposes people.

The first incident belongs to a very early stage in my life. My father was a free-thinker, but died when I was only three years old. Wishing me to be brought up without superstition, he appointed two free-thinkers as my guardians. The Courts, however, set aside his will, and had me educated in the Christian faith. I am afraid the result was disappointing, but that was not the fault of the law. If he had directed that I should be educated as a Christadelphian or a Muggletonian or a Seventh-Day Adventist, the Courts would not have dreamed of objecting. A parent has a right to ordain that any imaginable superstition shall be instilled into his children after his death, but has not the right to say that they shall be kept free from superstition if possible.

The second incident occurred in the year 1910. I had at that time a desire to stand for Parliament as a Liberal, and the Whips recommended me to a certain constituency. I addressed the Liberal Association, who expressed themselves favourably, and my adoption seemed certain. But being questioned by a small inner caucus, I admitted that I was an agnostic. They asked whether the fact would come out, and I said it probably would. They asked whether I should be willing to go to church occasionally, and I replied that I should not. Consequently they selected another candidate, who was duly elected, has been in Parliament ever since, and is a member of the present (1922) Government.

The third incident occurred immediately afterwards. I was invited by Trinity College, Cambridge, to become a lecturer, but not a Fellow. The difference is not pecuniary; it is that a Fellow has a voice in the government of the College, and cannot be dispossessed during the term of his Fellowship except for grave immorality. The reason for not offering me a Fellowship was that the clerical party did not wish to add to the anti-clerical vote. The result was that they were able to dismiss me in 1916, when they disliked my views on the war.[1] If I had been dependent on my lectureship, I should have starved.

These three incidents illustrate different kinds of disadvantages attaching to avowed free-thinking even in modern England. Any other avowed free-thinker could supply similar incidents from his personal experience, often of a far more serious character. The net result is that people who are not well-to-do dare not be frank about their religious beliefs.

It is not, of course, only or even chiefly in regard to religion that there is lack of freedom. Belief in Communism or free love handicaps a man much more than agnosticism. Not only is it a disadvantage to hold these views, but it is very much more difficult to obtain publicity for the arguments in their favour. On the other hand, in Russia the advantages and disadvantages are exactly reversed: comfort and power are achieved by professing atheism, Communism, and free love, and no opportunity exists for propaganda against these opinions. The result is that in Russia one set of fanatics feels absolute certainty about one set of doubtful propositions, while in the rest of the world another set of

[1] I should add that they reappointed me later, when war passions had begun to cool.

fanatics feels equal certainty about a diametrically opposite set of equally doubtful propositions. From such a situation war, bitterness, and persecution inevitably result on both sides.

William James used to preach the 'will to believe'. For my part, I should wish to preach the 'will to doubt'. None of our beliefs are quite true; all have at least a penumbra of vagueness and error. The methods of increasing the degree of truth in our beliefs are well known; they consist in hearing all sides, trying to ascertain all the relevant facts, controlling our own bias by discussion with people who have the opposite bias, and cultivating a readiness to discard any hypothesis which has proved inadequate. These methods are practised in science, and have built up the body of scientific knowledge. Every man of science whose outlook is truly scientific is ready to admit that what passes for scientific knowledge at the moment is sure to require correction with the progress of discovery; nevertheless, it is near enough to the truth to serve for most practical purposes, though not for all. In science, where alone something approximating to genuine knowledge is to be found, men's attitude is tentative and full of doubt.

In religion and politics, on the contrary, though there is as yet nothing approaching scientific knowledge, everybody considers it *de rigueur* to have a dogmatic opinion, to be backed up by inflicting starvation, prison, and war, and to be carefully guarded from argumentative competition with any different opinion. If only men could be brought into a tentatively agnostic frame of mind about these matters, nine-tenths of the evils of the modern world would be cured. War would become impossible, because each side would realise that both sides must be in the wrong. Persecution would cease. Education would aim at expanding the mind, not at narrowing it. Men would be chosen for jobs on account of fitness to do the work, not because they followed the irrational dogmas of those in power. Thus rational doubt alone, if it could be generated, would suffice to introduce the millennium.

We have had in recent years a brilliant example of the scientific temper of mind in the theory of relativity and its reception by the world. Einstein, a German-Swiss-Jew pacifist, was appointed to a research professorship by the German Government in the early days of the war; his predictions were verified by an English expedition which observed the eclipse of 1919, very soon after the Armistice. His theory upsets the whole theoretical framework of traditional physics; it is almost as damaging to orthodox dynamics as Darwin was to Genesis. Yet physicists everywhere have shown complete readiness to accept his theory as soon as it appeared that the evidence was in its favour. But none of them, least of all Einstein himself, would claim that he has said the last word. He has not built a monument of infallible dogma to stand for all time. There are difficulties he cannot solve; his doctrines will have to be modified in their turn as they have modified Newton's. This critical undogmatic receptiveness is the true attitude of science.

What would have happened if Einstein had advanced something equally new in the sphere of religion or politics? English people would have found elements of Prussianism in his theory; anti-Semites would have regarded it as a Zionist plot; nationalists in all countries would have found it tainted with lily-livered pacifism and proclaimed it a mere dodge for escaping military service. All the old-fashioned professors would have approached Scotland Yard to get the importation of his writings prohibited. Teachers favourable to him would have been dismissed. He, meantime, would have captured the Government of some backward country, where it would have become illegal to teach anything except his doctrine, which would have grown into a mysterious dogma not understood by anybody. Ultimately the truth or falsehood of his doctrine would be decided on the battlefield, without the collection of any fresh evidence for or against it. This method is the logical outcome of William James's will to believe.

What is wanted is not the will to believe, but the wish to find out, which is the exact opposite.

If it is admitted that a condition of rational doubt would be desirable, it becomes important to inquire how it comes about that there is so much irrational certainty in the world. A great deal of this is due to the inherent irrationality and credulity of average human nature. But this seed of intellectual original sin is nourished and fostered by other agencies, among which three play the chief part, namely, education, propaganda and economic pressure. Let us consider these in turn.

(1) *Education.* Elementary education, in all advanced countries, is in the hands of the State. Some of the things taught are known to be false by the officials who prescribe them, and many others are known to be false, or at any rate very doubtful, by

every unprejudiced person. Take, for example, the teaching of history. Each nation aims only at self-glorification in the school textbooks of history. When a man writes his autobiography he is expected to show a certain modesty; but when a nation writes its autobiography there is no limit to its boasting and vainglory. When I was young, schoolbooks taught that the French were wicked and the Germans virtuous; now they teach the opposite. In neither case is there the slightest regard for truth. German schoolbooks, dealing with the battle of Waterloo, represent Wellington as all but defeated when Blücher saved the situation; English books represent Blücher as having made very little difference. The writers of both the German and the English books know that they are not telling the truth. American school-books used to be violently anti-British; since the war they have become equally pro-British, without aiming at truth in either case.[1] Both before and since, one of the chief purposes of education in the United States has been to turn the motley collection of immigrant children into 'good Americans'. Apparently it has not occurred to anyone that a 'good American', like a 'good German', or a 'good Japanese', must be, *pro tanto*, a bad human being. A 'good American' is a man or woman imbued with the belief that America is the finest country on earth, and ought always to be enthusiastically supported in any quarrel. It is just possible that these propositions are true; if so, a rational man will have no quarrel with them. But if they are true, they ought to be taught everywhere, not only in America. It is a suspicious circumstance that such propositions are never believed outside the particular country which they glorify. Meanwhile the whole machinery of the State, in all the different countries, is turned on to making defenceless children believe absurd propositions, the effect of which is to make them willing to die in defence of sinister interests under the impression that they are fighting for truth and right. This is only one of the countless ways in which education is designed, not to give true knowledge, but to make the people pliable to the will of their masters. Without an elaborate system of deceit in the elementary schools it would be impossible to preserve the camouflage of democracy.

Before leaving the subject of education, I will take another example from America[2] – not because America is any worse than

[1] See *The Freeman*, February 15th, 1922, p. 532.
[2] See *The New Republic*, February 1st, 1922, pp. 259ff.

other countries, but because it is the most modern, showing the dangers that are growing rather than those that are diminishing. In the State of New York, a school cannot be established without a licence from the State, even if it is to be supported wholly by private funds. A recent law[1] decrees that a licence shall not be granted to any school 'where it shall appear that the instruction proposed to be given includes the teaching of the doctrine that organised governments shall be overthrown by force, violence, or unlawful means'. As the *New Republic* points out, there is no limitation to this or that organised Government. The law therefore should have made it illegal, during the war, to teach the doctrine that the Kaiser's Government should be overthrown by force; and since then, the support of Kolchak or Denikin against the Soviet Government would have been illegal. Such consequences, of course, were not intended, and result only from bad draughtsmanship. What was intended appears from another law passed at the same time, applying to teachers in State schools. This law provides that certificates permitting persons to teach in such schools shall only be issued to those who have 'shown satisfactorily' that they are 'loyal and obedient to the Government of this State and of the United States', and shall be refused to those who have advocated, no matter where or when, 'a form of government other than the Government of this State or of the United States'. The committee which framed these laws, as quoted by the *New Republic*, laid it down that the teacher who 'does not approve of the present social system ... must surrender his office', and that 'no person who is not eager to combat the theories of social change should be entrusted with the task of fitting the young and old for the responsibilities of citizenship'. Thus according to the law of the State of New York, Christ and George Washington were too degraded morally to be fit for the education of the young. If Christ were to go to New York and say, 'Suffer the little children to come unto me', the President of the New York School Board would reply: 'Sir, I see no evidence that you are eager to combat theories of social change. Indeed, I have heard it said that you advocate what you call the *kingdom* of heaven, whereas this country, thank God, is a republic. It is clear that the government of your kingdom of heaven would differ materially from that of New York State, therefore no children will be allowed access to you.' If he failed to

[1] Modified since the above was written.

make this reply, he would not be doing his duty as a functionary entrusted with the administration of the law.

The effect of such laws is very serious. Let it be granted, for the sake of argument, that the Government and the social system in the State of New York are the best that have ever existed on this planet; yet even then, both would presumably be capable of improvement. Any person who admits this obvious proposition is by law incapable of teaching in a State school. Thus the law decrees that the teachers shall all be either hypocrites or fools.

The growing danger exemplified by the New York law is that resulting from the monopoly of power in the hands of a single organisation, whether the State or a Trust or federation of Trusts. In the case of education, the power is in the hands of the State, which can prevent the young from hearing of any doctrine which it dislikes. I believe there are still some people who think that a democratic State is scarcely distinguishable from the people. This, however, is a delusion. The State is a collection of officials, different for different purposes, drawing comfortable incomes so long as the *status quo* is preserved. The only alteration they are likely to desire in the *status quo* is an increase of bureaucracy and of the power of bureaucrats. It is therefore natural that they should take advantage of such opportunities as war excitement to acquire inquisitorial powers over their employees, involving the right to inflict starvation upon any subordinate who opposes them. In matters of the mind, such as education, this state of affairs is fatal. It puts an end to all possibility of progress or freedom or intellectual initiative. Yet it is the natural result of allowing the whole of elementary education to fall under the sway of a single organisation.

Religious toleration, to a certain extent, has been won, because people have ceased to consider religion so important as it was once thought to be. But in politics and economics, which have taken the place formerly occupied by religion, there is a growing tendency to persecution, which is not by any means confined to one party. The persecution of opinion in Russia is more severe than in any capitalist country. I met in Petrograd an eminent Russian poet, Alexander Block, who has since died as the result of privations. The Bolsheviks allowed him to teach aesthetics, but he complained that they insisted on his teaching the subject 'from a Marxian point of view'. He had been at a loss to discover how the theory of rhythmics was connected with Marxism, although, to avoid starvation, he had done his best to find out. Of course it was impossible, in Russia, for years after the Bolsheviks came into power, to print anything critical of the dogmas upon which their régime is founded.

The examples of America and Russia illustrate the conclusion to which we seem to be driven, namely that, so long as men continue to have the present fanatical belief in the importance of politics, free thought on political matters will be impossible, and there is only too much danger that the lack of freedom will spread to all other matters, as it has done in Russia. Only some degree of political scepticism can save us from this misfortune.

It must not be supposed that the officials in charge of education desire the young to become educated. On the contrary, their problem is to impart information without imparting intelligence. Education should have two objects: first, to give definite knowledge, reading and writing, language and mathematics, and so on; secondly, to create those mental habits which will enable people to acquire knowledge and form sound judgements for themselves. The first of these we may call information, the second intelligence. The utility of information is admitted practically as well as theoretically; without a literate population a modern state is impossible. But the utility of intelligence is admitted only theoretically, not practically: it is not desired that ordinary people should think for themselves, because it is felt that people who think for themselves are awkward to manage and cause administrative difficulties. Only the guardians, in Plato's language, are to think; the rest are to obey, or to follow leaders like a herd of sheep. This doctrine, often unconsciously, has survived the introduction of political democracy, and has radically vitiated all national systems of education.

The country which has succeeded best in giving information without intelligence is the latest addition to modern civilisation, Japan. Elementary education in Japan is said to be admirable from the point of view of instruction. But in addition to instruction it has another purpose, which is to teach worship of the Mikado – a far stronger creed now than before Japan became modernised.[1] Thus the schools have been used simultaneously to

[1] See *The Invention of a New Religion*, by Professor Chamberlain of Tokyo. Published by the Rationalist Press Association.

confer knowledge and to promote superstition. Since we are not tempted to Mikado-worship, we see clearly what is absurd in Japanese teaching. Our own national superstitions strike us as natural and sensible, so that we do not take such a true view of them as we do of the superstitions of Nippon. But if a travelled Japanese were to maintain the thesis that our schools teach superstitions just as inimical to intelligence as belief in the divinity of the Mikado, I suspect that he would be able to make out a very good case.

For the present I am not in search of remedies, but am only concerned with diagnosis. We are faced with the paradoxical fact that education has become one of the chief obstacles to intelligence and freedom of thought. This is due primarily to the fact that the State claims a monopoly; but that is by no means the sole cause.

(2) *Propaganda.* Our system of education turns young people out of the schools able to read, but for the most part unable to weigh evidence or to form an independent opinion. They are then assailed, throughout the rest of their lives, by statements designed to make them believe all sorts of absurd propositions, such as that Blank's pills cure all ills, that Spitszbergen is warm and fertile, and that Germans eat corpses. The art of propaganda, as practised by modern politicians and governments, is derived from the art of advertisement. The science of psychology owes a great deal to advertisers. In former days, most psychologists would probably have thought that a man could not convince many people of the excellence of his own wares by merely stating emphatically that they were excellent. Experience shows, however, that they were mistaken in this. If I were to stand up once in a public place and state that I am the most modest man alive, I should be laughed at; but if I could raise enough money to make the same statement on all the buses and on hoardings along all the principal railway lines, people would presently become convinced that I had an abnormal shrinking from publicity. If I were to go to a small shopkeeper and say: 'Look at your competitor over the way: he is getting your business; don't you think it would be a good plan to leave your business and stand up in the middle of the road and try to shoot him before he shoots you?' – if I were to say this, any small shopkeeper would think me mad. But when the Government says it with emphasis and a brass band, the small shopkeepers become enthusiastic, and are quite surprised when they find afterwards

that business has suffered. Propaganda, conducted by the means which advertisers have found successful, is now one of the recognised methods of government in all advanced countries, and is especially the method by which democratic opinion is created.

There are two quite different evils about propaganda as now practised. On the one hand, its appeal is generally to irrational causes of belief rather than to serious argument; on the other hand, it gives an unfair advantage to those who can obtain most publicity, whether through wealth or through power. For my part, I am inclined to think that too much fuss is sometimes made about the fact that propaganda appeals to emotion rather than reason. The line between emotion and reason is not so sharp as some people think. Moreover, a clever man could frame a sufficiently rational argument in favour of any position which has any chance of being adopted. There are always good arguments on both sides of any real issue. Definite misstatements of fact can be legitimately objected to, but they are by no means necessary. The mere words 'Pears' Soap', which affirm nothing, cause people to buy that article. If, wherever these words appear, they were replaced by the words 'The Labour Party', millions of people would be led to vote for the Labour Party, although the advertisements had claimed no merit for it whatever. But if both sides in a controversy were confined by law to statements which a committee of eminent logicians considered relevant and valid, the main evil of propaganda, as at present conducted, would remain. Suppose, under such a law, two parties with an equally good case, one of whom had a million pounds to spend on propaganda while the other had only a hundred thousand. It is obvious that the arguments in favour of the richer party would become more widely known than those in favour of the poorer party, and therefore the richer party would win. This situation is of course intensified when one party is the Government. In Russia the Government has an almost complete monopoly of propaganda, but that is not necessary. The advantages which it possesses over its opponents will generally be sufficient to give it the victory, unless it has an exceptionally bad case.

The objection to propaganda is not only its appeal to unreason, but still more the unfair advantage which it gives to the rich and powerful. Equality of opportunity among opinions is essential if there is to be real freedom of thought; and equality of opportunity among opinions can only be secured by elaborate laws directed to that end, which there is no reason to expect to see enacted. The cure is not to be sought primarily in such laws, but in better education and a more sceptical public opinion. But for the moment I am not concerned to discuss cures.

(3) *Economic Pressure.* I have already dealt with some aspects of this obstacle to freedom of thought, but I wish now to deal with it on more general lines, as a danger which is bound to increase unless very definite steps are taken to counteract it. The supreme example of economic pressure applied against freedom of thought is Soviet Russia, where, until the trade agreement, the Government could and did inflict starvation upon people whose opinions it disliked, for example, Kropotkin. But in this respect Russia is only somewhat ahead of other countries. In France, during the Dreyfus affair, any teacher would have lost his position if he had been in favour of Dreyfus at the start or against him in the end. In America at the present day I doubt if a university professor, however eminent, could get employment if he were to criticise the Standard Oil Company, because all College Presidents have received or hope to receive benefactions from Mr Rockefeller. Throughout America socialists are marked men, and find it extremely difficult to obtain work unless they have great gifts. The tendency, which exists wherever industrialism is well developed, for trusts and monopolies to control all industry, leads to a diminution of the number of possible employers, so that it becomes easier and easier to keep secret black-books by means of which anyone not subservient to the great corporations can be starved. The growth of monopolies is introducing in America many of the evils associated with State Socialism as it has existed in Russia. From the standpoint of liberty, it makes no difference to a man whether his only possible employer is the State or a Trust.

In America, which is the most advanced country industrially, and to a lesser extent in other countries which are approximating to the American condition, it is necessary for the average citizen, if he wishes to make a living, to avoid incurring the hostility of certain big men. And these big men have an outlook – religious, moral and political – with which they expect their employees to agree, at least outwardly. A man who openly dissents from Christianity, or believes in a relaxation of the marriage laws, or objects

to the power of the great corporations, finds America a very uncomfortable country, unless he happens to be an eminent writer.
Exactly the same kind of restraints upon freedom of thought are
bound to occur in every country where economic organisation has
been carried to the point of practical monopoly. Therefore the
safeguarding of liberty in the world which is growing up is far
more difficult than it was in the nineteenth century, when free
competition was still a reality. Whoever cares about the freedom
of the mind must face this situation fully and frankly realising the
inapplicability of methods which answered well enough while industrialism was in its infancy.

There are two simple principles which, if they were adopted,
would solve almost all social problems. The first is that education
should have for one of its aims to teach people only to believe
propositions when there is some reason to think that they are true.
The second is that jobs should be given solely for fitness to do the
work.

To take the second point first: the habit of considering a man's
religious, moral and political opinions before appointing him to a
post or giving him a job is the modern form of persecution, and it
is likely to become quite as efficient as the Inquisition ever was.
The old liberties can be legally retained without being of the
slightest use. If, in practice, certain opinions lead a man to starve,
it is poor comfort to him to know that his opinions are not pun-
ishable by law. There is a certain public feeling against starving
men for not belonging to the Church of England, or for holding
slightly unorthodox opinions in politics. But there is hardly any
feeling against the rejection of atheists or Mormons, extreme
communists, or men who advocate free love. Such men are
thought to be wicked, and it is considered only natural to refuse to
employ them. People have hardly yet waked up to the fact that
this refusal, in a highly industrial State, amounts to a very vigorous form of persecution.

If this danger were adequately realised, it would be possible to
rouse public opinion, and to secure that a man's beliefs should not
be considered in appointing him to a post. The protection of minorities is vitally important; and even the most orthodox of us may
find himself in a minority some day, so that we all have an interest
in restraining the tyranny of majorities. Nothing except public
opinion can solve this problem. Socialism would make it somewhat

more acute, since it would eliminate the opportunities that now arise through exceptional employers. Every increase in the size of industrial undertakings makes it worse, since it diminishes the number of independent employers. The battle must be fought exactly as the battle of religious toleration was fought. And as in that case, so in this, a decay in the intensity of belief is likely to prove the decisive factor. While men were convinced of the absolute truth of Catholicism or Protestantism, as the case may be, they were willing to persecute on account of them. While men are quite certain of their modern creeds, they will persecute on their behalf. Some element of doubt is essential to the practice, though not to the theory, of toleration. And this brings me to my other point, which concerns the aims of education.

If there is to be toleration in the world, one of the things taught in schools must be the habit of weighing evidence, and the practice of not giving full assent to propositions which there is no reason to believe true. For example, the art of reading the newspapers should be taught. The schoolmaster should select some incident which happened a good many years ago, and roused political passions in its day. He should then read to the school-children what was said by the newspapers on one side, what was said by those on the other, and some impartial account of what really happened. He should show how, from the biased account of either side, a practised reader could infer what really happened, and he should make them understand that everything in newspapers is more or less untrue. The cynical scepticism which would result from this teaching would make the children in later life immune from those appeals to idealism by which decent people are induced to further the schemes of scoundrels.

History should be taught in the same way. Napoleon's campaigns of 1813 and 1814, for instance, might be studied in the *Moniteur*, leading up to the surprise which Parisians felt when they saw the Allies arriving under the walls of Paris after they had (according to the official bulletins) been beaten by Napoleon in every battle. In the more advanced classes, students should be encouraged to count the number of times that Lenin has been assassinated by Trotsky, in order to learn contempt for death. Finally, they should be given a school history approved by the Government, and asked to infer what a French school history would say about our wars with France. All this would be a far better training in citizenship than the trite moral maxims by which some people believe that civic duty can be inculcated.

It must, I think, be admitted that the evils of the world are due to moral defects quite as much as to lack of intelligence. But the human race has not hitherto discovered any method of eradicating moral defects; preaching and exhortation only add hypocrisy to the previous list of vices. Intelligence, on the contrary, is easily improved by methods known to every competent educator. Therefore, until some method of teaching virtue has been discovered, progress will have to be sought by improvement of intelligence rather than of morals. One of the chief obstacles to intelligence is credulity, and credulity could be enormously diminished by instruction in the prevalent forms of mendacity. Credulity is a greater evil in the present day than it ever was before, because, owing to the growth of education, it is much easier than it used to be to spread information, and owing to democracy, the spread of mis-information is more important than in former times to the holders of power. Hence the increase in the circulation of newspapers.

If I am asked how the world is to be induced to adopt these two maxims, namely, (1) that jobs should be given to people on account of their fitness to perform them, (2) that one aim of education should be to cure people of the habit of believing propositions for which there is no evidence, I can only say that it must be done by generating an enlightened public opinion. And an enlightened public opinion can only be generated by the efforts of those who desire that it should exist. I do not believe that the economic changes advocated by socialists will, of themselves, do anything towards curing the evils we have been considering. I think that, whatever happens in politics, the trend of economic development will make the preservation of mental freedom increasingly difficult, unless public opinion insists that the employer shall control nothing in the life of the employee except his work. Freedom in education could easily be secured, if it were desired, by limiting the function of the State to inspection and payment, and confining inspection rigidly to the definite instruction. But that, as things stand, would leave education in the hands of the churches, because, unfortunately, they are more anxious to teach their beliefs than free-thinkers are to teach their doubts. It would, however, give a free field, and would make it possible for a liberal education to be given if it were really desired. More than that ought not to be asked of the law.

My plea throughout this essay has been for the spread of the scientific temper, which is an altogether different thing from the knowledge of scientific results. The scientific temper is capable of regenerating mankind and providing an issue for all our troubles. The results of science, in the form of mechanism, poison gas and the Yellow Press, bid fair to lead to the total downfall of our civilisation. It is a curious antithesis, which a Martian might contemplate with amused detachment. But for us it is a matter of life and death. Upon its issue depends the question whether our grandchildren are to live in a happier world, or are to exterminate each other by scientific methods, leaving perhaps to negroes and Papuans the future destinies of mankind.

Chapter 13

Freedom in Society

To what extent is freedom possible, and to what extent is it desirable, among human beings who live in communities? That is the general problem which I wish to discuss.

Perhaps it will be well to begin with definitions. 'Freedom' is a term which is used in many senses, and we must decide upon one of them before we can argue profitably. 'Society' is less ambiguous, but here too some attempt at definition may be not amiss.

I do not think it desirable to use words in fancy senses. For instance, Hegel and his followers think that 'true' freedom consists in the right to obey the police, who are generally called 'the moral law'. The police, of course, must obey their official superiors, but the definition gives us no guidance as to what the Government itself is to do. Accordingly, in practice, the adherents of this view argue that the State is essentially and by definition impeccable. This notion is inappropriate in a country where there is democracy and party Government, since in such a country nearly half the nation believes the Government to be very wicked. We cannot therefore rest content with 'true' freedom as a substitute for freedom.

'Freedom' in its most abstract sense means the absence of external obstacles to the realisation of desires. Taken in this abstract sense, freedom may be increased either by maximising power or by minimising wants. An insect which lives for a few days and then dies of cold may have perfect freedom according to the definition, since the cold may alter its desires, so that there is no moment when it wishes to achieve the impossible. Among human beings, also, this way of reaching freedom is possible. A young Russian aristocrat, who had become a communist and a Red Army Commissar, explained to me that the English do not, like the Russians, need a physical strait-jacket, because they have a mental one: their souls are always in strait-jackets. Probably there is some truth in this. The people in Dostoevsky are no doubt not quite like real Russians, but at any rate they are people whom only a Russian could have invented. They have all sorts of strange violent desires, from which the average Englishman is free, at least so far as his conscious life is concerned. It is obvious that a community who all wish to murder each other cannot be so free as a community with more peaceable desires. Modification of desire may, therefore, involve just as great a gain to freedom as increase of power.

This consideration illustrates a necessity which is not always satisfied by political thinking: I mean the necessity of what may be called 'psychological dynamics'. It has been far too common to accept human nature as a datum in politics, to which external conditions have to be adapted. The truth is, of course, that external conditions modify human nature, and that harmony between the two is to be sought by a mutual interaction. A man taken from one environment and plunged suddenly into another may be by no means free, and yet the new environment may give freedom to those accustomed to it. We cannot therefore deal with freedom without taking account of the possibility of variable desires owing to changing environment. In some cases this makes the attainment of freedom more difficult, since a new environment, while satisfying old desires, may generate new ones which it cannot satisfy. This possibility is illustrated by the psychological effects of industrialism, which generates a host of new wants: a man may be discontented because he cannot afford a motor-car, and soon we shall all want private aeroplanes. And a man may be discontented because of unconscious wants. For instance, Americans need rest, but do not know it. I believe this to be a large part of the explanation of the crime wave in the United States.

Although men's desires vary, there are certain fundamental needs which may be taken as nearly universal: food, drink, health, clothing, housing, sex and parenthood are the chief of these. (Clothing and housing are not absolute necessaries in hot climates, but except in the tropics they must be included in the list.) Whatever else may be involved in freedom, certainly no person is free who is deprived of anything in the above list, which constitutes the bare minimum of freedom.

This brings us to the definition of 'society'. It is obvious that the above minimum of freedom can be better secured in a society than by a Robinson Crusoe; indeed, sex and parenthood are essentially social. One may define a 'society' as a group of persons who co-operate for certain common purposes. Where human beings are concerned, the most primitive social group is the family. Economic social groups come quite early; apparently groups which co-operate in war are not quite so primitive. In the modern world, economics and war are the main motives for social cohesion. Almost all of us are better able to satisfy our physical needs than we should be if we had no larger social unit than the family or the tribe, and in that sense society has served to increase freedom. It is thought, also, that an organised State makes us less likely to be killed by our enemies, but this is a doubtful proposition.

If we take a man's desires as a datum, i.e. if we ignore psychological dynamics, it is obvious that the obstacles to his freedom are of two sorts, physical and social. To take the crudest instance: the earth may not yield enough food for his sustenance, or other people may prevent him from obtaining the food. Society diminishes the physical obstacles to freedom, but creates social obstacles. Here, however, we are liable to go wrong through ignoring the effect of society upon desire. One may assume that ants and bees, though they live in well-organised societies, always do spontaneously the things that constitute their social duties. The same is true of most of the individuals among higher animals that are gregarious. According to Rivers, it is true of men in Melanesia. This seems to depend upon a high degree of suggestibility, and upon factors more or less akin to what happens in hypnotism. Men so constituted can co-operate without loss of freedom, and have little need of law. Oddly enough, though civilised men have a far more elaborate social organisation than savages have, they appear to be less social in their instincts: the effect of society upon their actions is more external than it is with savages. That is why they discuss the problem of freedom.

I do not, of course, wish to deny that social co-operation has an instinctive basis, even in the most civilised communities. People want to be like their neighbours, and to be liked by them; they imitate, and they catch prevalent moods by suggestion. Nevertheless, these factors seem to diminish in strength as men become more civilised. They are much stronger in schoolboys than in adults, and on the whole they have most power over the least intelligent individuals. More and more, social co-operation is coming to depend upon rational apprehension of its advantages, rather than upon what is loosely termed herd instinct. The problem of individual liberty does not arise among savages, because they feel no need of it, but it arises among civilised men with more and more urgency as they become more civilised. And at the same time the part played by government in the regulation of their lives is continually increasing, as it becomes more clear that government can help to liberate us from the physical obstacles to freedom. The problem of freedom in society is therefore one which is likely to increase in urgency, unless we cease to become more civilised.

It is, of course, obvious that freedom is not to be increased by a mere diminution of government. One man's desires are apt to be incompatible with another man's, so that anarchy means freedom for the strong and slavery for the weak. Without government, the human population of the globe could hardly be a tenth of what it is; it would be kept down by starvation and infant mortality. This would be to substitute a physical slavery far more severe than the worst social slavery to be found in civilised communities in normal times. The problem we have to consider is not how to do without government, but how to secure its advantages with the smallest possible interference with freedom. This means striking a balance between physical and social freedom. To put it crudely: how much more governmental pressure should we be prepared to endure in order to have more food or better health?

The answer to this question, in practice, turns upon a very simple consideration: are we to have the food and health, or is someone else? People in a siege, or in England in 1917, have been found willing to endure any degree of governmental pressure, because it was obvious that it was to everyone's advantage. But when one person is to have the governmental pressure and another person is to have the food, the question looks quite different. In this form we arrive at the issue between capitalism and Socialism. Advocates of capitalism are very apt to appeal to the sacred principles of liberty, which are all embodied in one maxim: *The fortunate must not be restrained in the exercise of tyranny over the unfortunate.*

Laissez-faire Liberalism, which was based upon this maxim, must not be confounded with anarchism. It invoked the law to prevent murder and armed insurrection on the part of the unfortunate; as long as it dared, it opposed trade unionism. But given this minimum of government action, it aimed at accomplishing the rest by economic power. Liberalism considered it proper for an employer to say to an employee: 'You shall die of hunger', but improper for the employee to retort, 'You shall die first, of a bullet'. It is obvious that, apart from legal pedantries, it is ridiculous to make a distinction between these two threats. Each equally infringes the elementary minimum of freedom, but not one more than the other. It was not only in the economic sphere that this inequality existed. The sacred principles of liberty were also invoked to justify the tyranny of husbands over wives and fathers over children; but it must be said that Liberalism tended to mitigate the first of these. The tyranny of fathers over children, in the form of compelling them to work in factories, was mitigated in spite of the Liberals.

But this is a well-worn theme, and I do not wish to linger on it. I want to pass to the general question: How far should the community interfere with the individual, not for the sake of another individual, but for the sake of the community? And for what objects should it interfere?

I should say, to begin with, that the claim to the bare minimum of freedom – food, drink, health, housing, clothing, sex and parenthood – should override any other claim. The above minimum is necessary for biological survival, i.e. for the leaving of descendants. The things which I have just enumerated may, therefore, be described as necessaries; what goes beyond them may be called comforts or luxuries according to circumstances. Now I should regard it as *a priori* justifiable to deprive one person of comforts in order to supply another with necessaries. It may not be politically expedient, it may not be economically feasible, in a given community at a given moment; but it is not objectionable on the ground of freedom, because to deprive a man of necessaries is a greater interference with freedom than to prevent him from accumulating superfluities.

But if this is admitted, it takes us very far. Consider health, for instance. In Borough Council elections one of the questions to be decided is the amount of public money to be spent on such matters as public health, maternity care and infant welfare. Statistics prove that what is spent on these objects has a remarkable effect in saving life. In every borough in London, the well-to-do have banded themselves together to prevent an increase, and if possible to secure a diminution, of the expenditure in these directions. That is to say, they are all prepared to condemn thousands of people to death in order that they themselves may continue to enjoy good dinners and motor-cars. As they control almost all the Press, they prevent the facts from being known to their victims. By the methods familiar to psycho-analysts, they avoid knowing the facts themselves. There is nothing surprising in their action, which is that of all aristocracies in all ages. All that I am concerned to say is that their action cannot be defended on grounds of freedom.

I do not propose to discuss the right to sex and parenthood. I will merely observe that, in a country where there is a great excess of one sex over the other, existing institutions seem hardly calculated to secure it; and that the tradition of Christian asceticism has had the unfortunate effect of making people less willing to recognise this right than to recognise the right to food. Politicians, who have not time to become acquainted with human nature, are peculiarly ignorant of the desires that move ordinary men and women. Any political party whose leaders knew a little psychology could sweep the country.

While admitting the abstract right of the community to interfere with its members in order to secure the biological necessaries to all, I cannot admit its right to interfere in matters where what one man possesses is not obtained at the expense of another. I am thinking of such things as opinion and knowledge and art. The fact that the majority of a community dislikes an opinion gives it no right to interfere with those who hold it. And the fact that the majority of a community wishes not to know certain facts gives it no right to imprison those who wish to know them. I know a lady who wrote a long book giving an account of family life in Texas, which I consider sociologically very valuable. The British police hold that no one must know the truth about anything; therefore it is illegal to send this book through the post. Everybody knows that the patients of psycho-analysts are often cured by the mere process of making them become aware of facts of which they had repressed the recollection. Society is, in certain respects, like these patients, but instead of allowing itself to be cured it imprisons the doctors who bring unwelcome facts to its notice. This is a wholly undesirable form of interference with freedom. The same argument applies to interferences with personal morals: if a man chooses to have two wives or a woman two husbands, it is his affair and theirs, and no one else ought to feel called upon to take action about it.

So far, I have been considering purely abstract arguments as to the limitations of justifiable interferences with freedom. I come now to certain more psychological considerations.

The obstacles to freedom, as we saw, are of two sorts, social and physical. Given a social and a physical obstacle which cause the same direct loss of liberty, the social obstacle is more harmful, because it causes resentment. If a boy wants to climb a tree and you forbid him, he will be furious; if he finds that he cannot climb it, he will acquiesce in the physical impossibility. To prevent resentment, it may often be desirable to permit things which are in themselves harmful, such as going to church during an epidemic. To prevent resentment, governments attribute misfortunes to natural causes; to create resentment, oppositions attribute them to human causes. When the price of bread goes up, governments say it is due to bad harvests, and oppositions say it is due to profiteers. Under the influence of industrialism, people have come to believe more and more in the omnipotence of man; they think there is no limit to what human beings can do to obviate natural misfortunes. Socialism is a form of this belief: we no longer regard poverty as sent by God, but as a result of human folly and cruelty. This has naturally altered the attitude of the proletariat towards its 'betters'. Sometimes the belief in human omnipotence is carried too far. Many socialists, including the late Health Minister, apparently think that under Socialism there would be plenty of food for everybody even if the population multiplied until there was only standing room on the earth's surface. This, I am afraid, is an exaggeration. However this may be, the modern belief in the omnipotence of man has increased the resentment when things go wrong, because misfortunes are no longer attributed to God or Nature, even when they justly might be. This makes modern communities harder to govern than the communities of the past, and accounts for the fact that the governing classes tend to be exceptionally religious, because they wish to regard the misfortunes of their victims as due to the will of God. It makes interferences with the minimum of freedom harder to justify than in former times, because they cannot be camouflaged as immutable laws, although every day in *The Times* there are letters from clergymen trying to revive this ancient device.

In addition to the fact that interferences with social freedom are resented, there are two other reasons which tend to make them undesirable. The first is that people do not desire the welfare of others, and the second is that they do not know in what it consists. Perhaps, at bottom, these are one and the same, for when we genuinely desire the good of some person, we usually succeed in finding out what his needs are. At any rate, the practical results are the same whether people do harm from malevolence or from ignorance. We may therefore take the two together, and say that hardly any man or class can be trusted as the trustee of another's interests. This is, of course, the basis of the argument for democracy. But democracy, in a modern State, has to work through officials, and thus becomes indirect and remote where the individual is concerned. There is a special danger in officials, owing to the fact that they usually sit in offices remote from the people whose lives they control. Take education as a case in point. Teachers, on the whole, from contact with children, have come to understand them and care for them, but they are controlled by officials without practical experience, to whom children may be merely nasty little brats. Therefore the interferences of officials with freedom for teachers are generally harmful. So in everything: power lies with those who control finance, not with those who know the matter upon which the money is to be spent. Thus the holders of power are, in general, ignorant and malevolent, and the less they exercise their power the better.

The case for compulsion is strongest where the person compelled gives a moral assent to the compulsion, although, if he could, he would neglect what he recognises to be his duty. We would all rather pay rates than have no roads, though if, by a miracle, the rate-collector overlooked us, most of us would not remind him of our existence. And we readily acquiesce in such measures as the prohibition of cocaine, though alcohol is a more dubious proposition. But the best case is that of children. Children must be under authority, and are themselves aware that they must be, although they like to play a game of rebellion at times. The case of children is unique in the fact that those who have authority over them are sometimes fond of them. Where this is the case, the children do not resent the authority in general, even when they resist it on particular occasions. Education authorities, as opposed to teachers, have not this merit, and do in fact sacrifice the children to what they consider the good of the State by teaching them 'patriotism', i.e. a willingness to kill and be killed for trivial reasons. Authority would be comparatively harmless if it were always in the hands of people who wish well to those whom they control, but there is no known method of securing this result.

Compulsion is at its worst when the victim firmly believes the act commanded to be wicked or harmful. It would be abominable, even if it were possible, to compel a Mahometan to eat pork or a Hindu to eat beef. Anti-vaccinationists ought not to be compelled to be vaccinated. Whether their infant children should be is another question: I should say not, but the question is not one of freedom, since the child is not consulted in either case. The question is one between the parent and the State, and cannot be decided on any general principle. The parent who has conscientious objections to education is not allowed to keep his child uninstructed; yet, so far as general principles go, the two cases are exactly analogous.

The most important distinction, in this matter of freedom, is between those goods which one man holds at the expense of another, and those in which one man's gain is not another's loss. If I absorb more than my fair share of food, some other man goes hungry; if I absorb an unusually large amount of mathematics, I do no one any harm, unless I have monopolised educational opportunities. There is another point: such things as food, houses and clothes are necessaries of life, about the need of which there is not much controversy or much difference between one man and another. Therefore they are suitable for governmental action in a democracy. In all such matters justice should be the governing principle. In a modern democratic community, justice means equality. But it would not mean equality in a community where there was a hierarchy of classes, recognised and accepted by inferiors as well as superiors. Even in modern England, a large majority of wage-earners would be shocked if it were suggested that the King should have no more pomp than they have. I should therefore define justice as the arrangement of producing the least envy. This would mean equality in a community free from superstition, but not in one which firmly believed in social inequality.

But in opinion, thought, art, etc., one man's possessions are not obtained at the expense of another's. Moreover, it is doubtful what is good in this sphere. If Dives is having a feast while Lazarus is eating a crust of bread, Dives will be thought a hypocrite if he preaches the advantages of poverty. But if I like mathematics and another man likes music, we do not interfere with each other, and when we praise each other's pursuits we are merely being polite. And in matters of opinion, free competition is the only way of arriving at truth. The old Liberal watchwords were applied in the wrong sphere, that of economics; it is in the mental sphere that they really apply. We want free competition in ideas, not in business. The difficulty is that, as free competition in business dies out, the victors more and more seek to use their economic power in the mental and moral sphere, and to insist upon right living and right thinking as a condition of being allowed to earn a living. This is unfortunate, since 'right living' means hypocrisy and 'right thinking' means stupidity. There is the gravest danger that, whether under plutocracy or under Socialism, all mental and moral progress will be rendered impossible by economic persecution. The liberty of the individual should be respected where his actions do not directly, obviously and indubitably do harm to other people. Otherwise our persecuting instincts will produce a stereotyped society, as in sixteenth-century Spain. The danger is real and pressing. America is in the van, but we in England are almost sure to follow suit, unless we can learn to value freedom in its proper sphere. The freedom we should seek is not the right to oppress others, but the right to live as we choose and think as we choose where our doing so does not prevent others from doing likewise.

Finally, I want to say a word about what, at the beginning, I called 'psychological dynamics'. A society where one type of character is common can have more freedom than one in which a different type prevails. A society composed of human beings and tigers could not have much freedom: either the tigers or the human beings must be enslaved. There cannot therefore be any freedom in parts of the world where white men govern coloured populations. To secure the maximum of freedom, it is necessary to form character by education, so that men may find their happiness in activities which are not oppressive. This is a matter of formation of character during the first six years of life. Miss McMillan at Deptford is training children who become capable of creating a free community. If her methods were applied to all children, rich and poor, one generation would suffice to solve our social problems.

But emphasis on instruction has made all parties blind to what is important in education. In later years, desires can only be controlled, not fundamentally altered; therefore it is in early childhood that the lesson of live-and-let-live must be taught. Given men and woman who do not desire the things which can only be secured through the misfortunes of others, the obstacles to social freedom will be at an end.

Chapter 14

Freedom Versus Authority in Education

Freedom, in education as in other things, must be a matter of degree. Some freedoms cannot be tolerated. I met a lady once who maintained that no child should ever be forbidden to do anything, because a child ought to develop its nature from within. 'How if its nature leads it to swallow pins?' I asked; but I regret to say the answer was mere vituperation. And yet every child, left to itself, will sooner or later swallow pins, or drink poison out of medicine bottles, or fall out of an upper window, or otherwise bring itself to a bad end. At a slightly later age, boys, when they have the opportunity, will go unwashed, overeat, smoke till they are sick, catch chills from sitting in wet feet, and so on – let alone the fact that they will amuse themselves by plaguing elderly gentlemen, who may not all have Elisha's powers of repartee. Therefore one who advocates freedom in education cannot mean that children should do exactly as they please all day long. An element of discipline and authority must exist; the question is as to the amount of it, and the way in which it is to be exercised.

Education may be viewed from many standpoints: that of the State, of the Church, of the schoolmaster, of the parents, or even (though this is usually forgotten) of the child itself. Each of these points of view is partial; each contributes something to the ideal of education, but also contributes elements that are bad. Let us examine them successively, and see what is to be said for and against them.

We will begin with the State, as the most powerful force in deciding what modern education is to be. The interest of the State in education is very recent. It did not exist in antiquity or the Middle Ages; until the Renaissance, education was only valued by the Church. The Renaissance brought an interest in advanced scholarship, leading to the foundation of such institutions as the

Collège de France, intended to offset the ecclesiastical Sorbonne. The Reformation, in England and Germany, brought a desire on the part of the State to have some control over universities and grammar schools, to prevent them from remaining hotbeds of 'Popery'. But this interest soon evaporated. The State took no decisive or continuous part until the quite modern movement for universal compulsory education. Nevertheless the State, now, has more to say to scholastic institutions than have all the other factors combined.

The motives which led to universal compulsory education were various. Its strongest advocates were moved by the feeling that it is in itself desirable to be able to read and write, that an ignorant population is a disgrace to a civilised country, and that democracy is impossible without education. These motives were reinforced by others. It was soon seen that education gave commercial advantages, that it diminished juvenile crime, and that it gave opportunities for regimenting slum populations. Anti-clericals perceived in State education an opportunity of combating the influence of the Church; this motive weighed considerably in England and France. Nationalists, especially after the Franco-Prussion War, considered that universal education would increase the national strength. All these other reasons, however, were at first subsidiary. The main reason for adopting universal education was the feeling that illiteracy was disgraceful.

This institution, once firmly established, was found by the State to be capable of many uses. It makes young people more docile, both for good and evil. It improves manners and diminishes crime; it facilitates common action for public ends; it makes the community more responsive to direction from a centre. Without it, democracy cannot exist except as an empty form. But democracy, as conceived by politicians, is a form of *government*, that is to say, it is a method of making people do what their leaders wish under the impression that they are doing what they themselves wish. Accordingly, State education has acquired a certain bias. It teaches the young (so far as it can) to respect existing institutions, to avoid all fundamental criticism of the powers that be, and to regard foreign nations with suspicion and contempt. It increases national solidarity at the expense both of internationalism and of individual development. The damage to individual development comes through the undue stress upon authority. Collective rather than individual emotions are encouraged, and disagreement with prevailing beliefs is severely repressed. Uniformity is desired because it is convenient to the administrator, regardless of the fact that it can only be secured by mental atrophy. So great are the resulting evils that it can be seriously questioned whether universal education has hitherto done good or harm on the balance.

The point of view of the Church as regards education is, in practice, not very different from that of the State. There is, however, one important divergence: the Church would prefer that the laity should not be educated at all, and only give them instruction when the State insists. The State and the Church both wish to instil beliefs which are likely to be dispelled by free inquiry. But the State creed is easier to instil into a population which can read the newspaper, whereas the Church creed is easier to instil into a wholly illiterate population. State and Church are both hostile to thought, but the Church is also (though now surreptitiously) hostile to instruction. This will pass, and is passing, as the ecclesiastical authorities perfect the technique of giving instruction without stimulating mental activity – a technique in which, long ago, the Jesuits led the way.

The schoolmaster, in the modern world, is seldom allowed a point of view of his own. He is appointed by an education authority, and is 'sacked' if he is found to be educating. Apart from this economic motive, the schoolmaster is exposed to temptations of which he is likely to be unconscious. He stands, even more directly than the State and the Church, for discipline; officially he knows what his pupils do not know. Without some element of discipline and authority, it is difficult to keep a class in order. It is easier to punish a boy for showing boredom than it is to be interesting. Moreover, even the best schoolmaster is likely to exaggerate his importance, and to deem it possible and desirable to mould his pupils into the sort of human beings that he thinks they ought to be. Lytton Strachey describes Dr Arnold walking beside the Lake of Como and meditating on 'moral evil'. Moral evil, for him, was whatever he wished to change in his boys. The belief that there was a great deal of it in them justified him in the exercise of power, and in conceiving of himself as a ruler whose duty was even more to chasten than to love. This attitude – variously phrased in various ages – is natural to any schoolmaster who is zealous without being on the watch for the deceitful influence of self-importance. Nevertheless the teacher is far the best of the forces concerned in education, and it is primarily to him or her that we must look for progress.

Then again, the schoolmaster wants the credit of his school. This makes him wish to have his boys distinguish themselves in athletic contests and scholarship examinations, which leads to care for a certain selection of superior boys to the exclusion of others. For the rank and file, the result is bad. It is much better for a boy to play a game badly himself than to watch others playing it well. Mr H. G. Wells, in his *Life of Sanderson of Oundle*, tells how this really great schoolmaster set his face against everything that left the faculties of the average boy unexercised and uncared-for. When he became headmaster, he found that only certain selected boys were expected to sing in chapel; they were trained as a choir, and the rest listened. Sanderson insisted that all should sing, whether musical or not. In this he was rising above the bias which is natural to a schoolmaster who cares more for his credit than for his boys. Of course, if we all apportioned credit wisely there would be no conflict between these two motives: the school which did best by the boys would get the most credit. But in a busy world spectacular successes will always win credit out of proportion to their real importance, so that some conflict between the two motives is hardly avoidable.

I come now to the point of view of the parent. This differs according to the economic status of the parent: the average wage-earner has desires quite different from those of the average professional man. The average wage-earner wishes to get his children to school as soon as possible, so as to diminish bother at home; he also wishes to get them away as soon as possible, so as to profit by their earnings. When recently the British Government decided to cut down expenditure on education, it proposed that children should not go to school before the age of six, and should not be obliged to stay after the age of thirteen. The former proposal caused such a popular outcry that it had to be dropped: the indignation of worried mothers (recently enfranchised) was irresistible. The latter proposal, lowering the age for leaving school, was not unpopular. Parliamentary candidates advocating better education would get unanimous applause from those who came to meetings, but would find, in canvassing, that unpolitical wage-earners (who are the majority) want their children to be free to get paid work as soon as possible. The exceptions are mainly those who hope that their children may rise in the social scale through better education.

Professional men have quite a different outlook. Their own income depends upon the fact that they have had a better education than the average, and they wish to hand on this advantage to their children. For this object they are willing to make great sacrifices. But in our present competitive society, what will be desired by the average parent is not an education which is good in itself, but an education which is better than other people's. This may be facilitated by keeping down the general level, and therefore we cannot expect a professional man to be enthusiastic about facilities for higher education for the children of wage-earners. If everybody who desired it could get a medical education, however poor his parents might be, it is obvious that doctors would earn less than they do, both from increased competition and from the improved health of the community. The same thing applies to the law, the civil service, and so on. Thus the good things which the professional man desires for his own children he will not desire for the bulk of the population unless he has exceptional public spirit.

The fundamental defect of fathers, in our competitive society, is that they want their children to be a credit to them. This is rooted in instinct, and can only be cured by efforts directed to that end. The defect exists also, though to a lesser degree, in mothers. We all feel instinctively, that our children's successes reflect glory upon ourselves, while their failures make us feel shame. Unfortunately, the successes which cause us to swell with pride are often of an undesirable kind. From the dawn of civilisation till almost our own time – and still in China and Japan – parents have sacrificed their children's happiness in marriage by deciding whom they were to marry, choosing almost always the richest bride or bridegroom available. In the western world (except partially in France) children have freed themselves from this slavery by rebellion, but parents' instincts have not changed. Neither happiness nor virtue, but worldly success, is what the average father desires for his children. He wants them to be such as he can boast of to his cronies, and this desire largely dominates his efforts for their education.

Authority, if it is to govern education, must rest upon one or several of the powers we have considered: the State, the Church, the schoolmaster and the parent. We have seen that no one of them can be trusted to care adequately for the child's welfare, since each wishes the child to minister to some end which has nothing to do with its own well-being. The State wants the child to serve for national aggrandisement and the support of the existing form of government. The Church wants the child to serve for increasing the power of the priesthood. The schoolmaster, in a competitive world, too often regards his school as the State regards the nation, and wants the child to glorify the school. The parent wants the child to glorify the family. The child itself, as an end in itself, as a separate human being with a claim to whatever happiness and well-being may be possible, does not come into these various external purposes, except very partially. Unfortunately, the child lacks the experience required for the guidance of its own life, and is therefore a prey to the sinister interests that batten on its innocence. This is what makes the difficulty of education as a political problem. But let us first see what can be said from the child's own point of view.

It is obvious that most children, if they were left to themselves, would not learn to read or write, and would grow up less adapted than they might be to the circumstances of their lives. There must be educational institutions, and children must be to some extent under authority. But in view of the fact that no authority can be wholly trusted, we must aim at having as little authority as possible, and try to think out ways by which young people's natural desires and impulses can be utilised in education. This is far more possible than is often thought, for, after all, the desire to acquire knowledge is natural to most young people. The traditional pedagogue, possessing knowledge not worth imparting, and devoid of all skill in imparting it, imagined that young people have a native horror of instruction, but in this he was misled by failure to realise his own shortcomings. There is a charming tale of Tchekov's about a man who tried to teach a kitten to catch mice. When it wouldn't run after them, he beat it, with the result that even as an adult cat, it cowered with terror in the presence of a mouse. 'This is the man,' Tchekov adds, 'who taught me Latin.' Now cats teach their kittens to catch mice, but they wait till the instinct has awakened. Then the kittens agree with their mammas that the knowledge is worth acquiring, so that discipline is not required.

The first two or three years of life have hitherto escaped the domination of the pedagogue, and all authorities are agreed that those are the years in which we learn most. Every child learns to talk by its own efforts. Anyone who has watched an infant knows that the efforts required are very considerable. The child listens intently, watches movements of the lips, practises sounds all day long, and concentrates with amazing ardour. Of course grown-up people encourage it by praise, but it does not occur to them to punish it on days when it learns no new word. All that they provide is opportunity and praise. It is doubtful whether more is required at any stage.

What is necessary is to make the child or young person feel that the knowledge is worth having. Sometimes this is difficult because in fact the knowledge is not worth having. It is also difficult when only a considerable amount of knowledge in any direction is useful, so that at first the pupil tends to be merely bored. In such cases, however, the difficulty is not insuperable. Take, for instance, the teaching of mathematics. Sanderson of Oundle found that almost all his boys were interested in machinery, and he provided them with opportunities for making quite elaborate machines. In the course of this practical work, they came upon the necessity for making calculations, and thus grew interested in mathematics as required for the success of a constructive enterprise on which they were keen. This method is expensive, and involves patient skill on the part of the teacher. But it goes along the lines of the pupil's instinct, and is therefore likely to involve less boredom with more intellectual effort. Effort is natural both to animals and men, but it must be effort for which there is an instinctive stimulus. A football match involves more effort than the treadmill, yet the one is a pleasure and the other a punishment. It is a mistake to suppose that mental effort can rarely be a pleasure; what is true is that certain conditions are required to make it pleasurable, and that, until lately, no attempt was made to create these conditions in education. The chief conditions are: first, a problem of which the solution is desired; secondly, a feeling of hopefulness as to the possibility of obtaining a solution. Consider the way David Copperfield was taught Arithmetic:

'Even when the lessons are done, the worst is yet to happen, in the shape of an appalling sum. This is invented for me, and delivered to me orally by Mr Murdstone, and begins, "If I go into a cheese-monger's shop, and buy five thousand double-Gloucester cheeses at fourpence-halfpenny each, present payment" – at which I see Miss Murdstone secretly overjoyed. I pore over these cheeses without any result or enlightenment until dinner-time; when, having made a mulatto of myself by getting the dirt of the slate into the pores of my skin, I have a slice of bread to help me out with the cheeses, and am considered in disgrace for the rest of the evening.'

Obviously the poor boy could not be expected to take any interest in the cheeses, or to have any hope of doing the sum right. If he had wanted a box of a certain size, and had been told to save up his allowance until he could buy enough wood and nails, it would have stimulated his arithmetical powers amazingly.

There should be nothing hypothetical about the sums that a child is asked to do. I remember once reading a young boy's own account of his arithmetic lesson. The governess set the problem: If a horse is worth three times as much as a pony, and the pony is worth £22, what is the horse worth? 'Had he been down?' asks the boy. 'That makes no difference,' says the governess. 'Oh, but James (the groom) says it makes a great difference.' The power of understanding hypothetical truth is one of the latest developments of logical faculty, and ought not to be expected in the very young. This, however, is a digression, from which we must return to our main theme.

I do not maintain that *all* children can have their intellectual interests aroused by suitable stimuli. Some have much less than average intelligence, and require special treatment. It is very un-desirable to combine in one class children whose mental capacities are very different: the cleverer ones will be bored by having things explained that they clearly understand, and the stupider ones will be worried by having things taken for granted that they have not yet grasped. But subjects and methods should be adapted to the intelligence of the pupil. Macaulay was made to learn mathematics at Cambridge, but it is obvious from his letters that it was a sheer waste of time. I was made to learn Latin and Greek, but I resented it, being of opinion that it was silly to learn a language that was no longer spoken. I believe that all the little good I got from years of classical studies I could have got in adult life in a month. After the bare minimum, account should be taken of tastes, and pupils should only be taught what they find interesting. This puts a strain upon teachers, who find it easier to be dull, especially if they are over-worked. But the difficulties can be overcome by giving teachers shorter hours and instruction in the art of teaching, which is done at present in training teachers in elementary schools, but not teachers in universities or public schools.

Freedom in education has many aspects. There is first of all freedom to learn or not to learn. Then there is freedom as to what to learn. And in later education there is freedom of opinion. Freedom to learn or not to learn can be only partially conceded in childhood. It is necessary to make sure that all who are not imbecile learn to read and write. How far this can be done by the mere provision of opportunity, only experience can show. But even if opportunity alone suffices, children must have the opportunity thrust upon them. Most of them would rather play out of doors, where the necessary opportunities would be lacking. Later on, it might be left to the choice of young people whether, for instance, they should go to the university; some would wish to do so, others would not. This would make quite as good a principle of selection as any to be got from entrance examinations. Nobody who did not work should be allowed to stay at a university. The rich young men who now waste their time in college are demoralising others and teaching themselves to be useless. If hard work were exacted as a condition of residence, universities would cease to be attractive to people with a distaste for intellectual pursuits.

Freedom as to what to learn ought to exist far more than at present. I think it is necessary to group subjects by their natural affinities; there are grave disadvantages in the elective system, which leaves a young man free to choose wholly unconnected subjects. If I were organising education in Utopia, with unlimited funds, I should give every child, at the age of about twelve, some instruction in classics, mathematics, and science. After two years, it ought to be evident where the child's aptitudes lay, and the child's own tastes would be a safe indication, provided there were no 'soft options'. Consequently I should allow every boy and girl who so desired to specialise from the age of fourteen. At first, the specialisation would be very broad, growing gradually more defined as education advanced. The time when it was possible to be universally well-informed is past. An industrious man may know something of history and literature, which requires a knowledge of classical and modern languages. Or he may know some parts of mathematics, or one or two sciences. But the ideal of an 'all-round' education is out of date; it has been destroyed by the progress of knowledge.

Freedom of opinion, on the part of both teachers and pupils, is the most important of the various kinds of freedom, and the only one which requires no limitations whatever. In view of the fact that it does not exist, it is worth while to recapitulate the arguments in its favour.

The fundamental argument for freedom of opinion is the doubtfulness of all our beliefs. If we certainly knew the truth, there would be something to be said for teaching it. But in that case it could be taught without invoking authority, by means of its inherent reasonableness. It is not necessary to make a law that no one shall be allowed to teach arithmetic if he holds heretical opinions on the multiplication table, because here the truth is clear, and does not require to be enforced by penalties. When the State intervenes to ensure the teaching of some doctrine, it does so *because* there is no conclusive evidence in favour of that doctrine. The result is that the teaching is not truthful, even if it should happen to be true. In the State of New York, it was till lately illegal to teach that Communism is good; in Soviet Russia, it is illegal to teach that Communism is bad. No doubt one of these opinions is true and one false, but no one knows which. Either New York or Soviet Russia was teaching truth and proscribing falsehood, but neither was teaching truthfully, because each was representing a doubtful proposition as certain.

The difference between truth and truthfulness is important in this connection. Truth is for the gods; from our point of view, it is an ideal, towards which we can approximate, but which we cannot hope to reach. Education should fit us for the nearest possible approach to truth, and to do this it must teach truthfulness. Truthfulness, as I mean it, is the habit of forming our opinions on the evidence, and holding them with that degree of conviction which the evidence warrants. This degree will always fall short of complete certainty, and therefore we must be always ready to admit new evidence against previous beliefs. Moreover, when we act on a belief, we must, if possible, only take such action as will be useful even if our belief is more or less inaccurate; we should avoid actions which are disastrous unless our belief is *exactly* true. In science, an observer states his results along with the 'probable error'; but who ever heard of a theologian or a politician stating the probable error in his dogmas, or even admitting that any error is conceivable? That is because in science, where we approach nearest to real knowledge, a man can safely rely on the strength of his case, whereas, where nothing is known, blatant assertion and hypnotism are the usual ways of causing others to share our beliefs. If the fundamentalists thought they had a good case against evolution, they would not make the teaching of it illegal.

The habit of teaching some one orthodoxy, political, religious, or moral, has all kinds of bad effects. To begin with, it excludes from the teaching profession men who combine honesty with intellectual vigour, who are just the men likely to have the best moral and mental effect upon their pupils. I will give three illustrations. First, as to politics: a teacher of economics in America is expected to teach such doctrines as will add to the wealth and power of the very rich; if he does not, he finds it advisable to go elsewhere, like Mr Laski, formerly of Harvard, now one of the most valuable teachers in the London School of Economics. Second, as to religion: the immense majority of intellectually eminent men disbelieve the Christian religion, but they conceal the fact in public, because they are afraid of losing their incomes. Thus on the most important of all subjects most of the men whose opinions and arguments would be best worth having are condemned to silence. Third, as to morals: Practically all men are unchaste at some time of their lives; clearly those who conceal this fact are worse than those who do not, since they add the guilt of hypocrisy. But it is only to the hypocrites that teaching posts are open. So much for the effects of orthodoxy upon the choice and character of teachers.

I come now to the effect upon the pupils, which I will take under two heads, intellectual and moral. Intellectually, what is stimulating to a young man is a problem of obvious practical importance, as to which he finds that divergent opinions are held. A young man learning economics, for example, ought to hear lectures from individualists and socialists, protectionists and free-traders, inflationists and believers in the gold standard. He ought to be encouraged to read the best books of the various schools, as recommended by those who believe in them. This would teach him to weigh arguments and evidence, to know that no opinion is certainly right, and to judge men by their quality rather than by their consonance with preconceptions. History should be taught not only from the point of view of one's own country, but also from that of foreigners. If history were taught by Frenchmen in England, and by Englishmen in France, there would be no disagreements between the two countries, each would understand the other's point of view. A young man should learn to think that all questions are open, and that an argument should be followed wherever it leads. The needs of practical life will destroy this attitude all too soon when he begins to earn his living; but until that time he should be encouraged to taste the joys of free speculation.

Morally, also, the teaching of an orthodoxy to the young is very harmful. There is not only the fact that it compels the abler teachers to be hypocrites, and therefore to set a bad moral example. There is also, what is more important, the fact that it encourages intolerance and the bad forms of herd instinct. Edmund Gosse, in his *Father and Son*, relates how, when he was a boy, his father told him he was going to marry again. The boy saw there was something his father was ashamed of, so at last he asked, in accents of horror: 'Father, is she a Paedo-Baptist?' And she was. Until that moment, he had believed all Paedo-Baptists to be wicked. So children in Catholic schools believe that Protestants are wicked, children in any school in an English-speaking country believe that atheists are wicked, children in France believe that Germans are wicked, and children in Germany believe that Frenchmen are wicked. When a school accepts as part of its task the teaching of an opinion which cannot be intellectually defended (as practically all schools do), it is compelled to give the impression that those who hold an opposite opinion are wicked, since otherwise it cannot generate the passion required for repelling the assaults of reason. Thus for the sake of orthodoxy the children are rendered uncharitable, intolerant, cruel, and bellicose. This is unavoidable so long as definite opinions are prescribed on politics, morals, and religion.

Finally, arising out of this moral damage to the individual, there is untold damage to society. Wars and persecutions are rife everywhere, and everywhere they are rendered possible by the teaching in the schools. Wellington used to say that the battle of Waterloo was won on the playing-fields of Eton. He might have said with more truth that the war against revolutionary France was instigated in the classrooms of Eton. In our democratic age, Eton has become unimportant; now, it is the ordinary elementary and secondary school that matters. In every country, by means of flag-waving, Empire Day, Fourth-of-July celebrations, Officer's Training Corps, etc., everything is done to give boys a taste for homicide, and girls a conviction that men given to homicide are the most worthy of respect. This whole system of moral degradation to which innocent boys and girls are exposed would become impossible if the authorities allowed freedom of opinion to teachers and pupils.

Regimentation is the source of the evil. Education authorities do not look on children, as religion is supposed to do, as human beings with souls to be saved. They look upon them as material for grandiose social schemes: future 'hands' in factories or 'bayonets' in war or what not. No man is fit to educate unless he feels each pupil an end in himself, with his own rights and his own personality, not merely a piece in a jig-saw puzzle, or a soldier in a regiment, or a citizen in a State. Reverence for human personality is the beginning of wisdom, in every social question, but above all in education.

Chapter 15

Psychology and Politics

I want to discuss in this essay the kind of effects which psychology may, before long, come to have upon politics. I propose to speak both of the good effects that are possible, and of the bad effects that are probable.

Political opinions are not based upon reason. Even so technical a matter as the resumption of the gold standard was determined mainly by sentiment, and according to the psycho-analysts, the sentiment in question is one which cannot be mentioned in polite society. Now the sentiments of an adult are compounded of a kernel of instinct surrounded by a vast husk of education. One way in which education works is through influencing imagination. Everybody wants to see himself as a fine fellow, and therefore both his efforts and his delusions are influenced by what he considers the best possible in the way of achievement. I think the study of psychology may alter our conception of a 'fine fellow'; if so, obviously its effect upon politics will be profound. I doubt whether anyone who had learnt modern psychology in youth could be quite like the late Lord Curzon or the present Bishop of London.

With regard to any science, there are two kinds of effects which it may have. On the one hand, experts may make inventions or discoveries which can be utilised by the holders of power. On the other hand, the science may influence imagination, and so alter people's analogies and expectations. There is, strictly speaking, a third kind of effect, namely a change in manner of life with all its consequences. In the case of physical science, all three classes of effects are, by this time, clearly developed. The first is illustrated by aeroplanes, the second by the mechanistic outlook on life, the third by the substitution, in a large part of the population, of industry and urban life for agriculture and the country. In the case of psychology, we still have to depend upon prophecy as regards most of its effects. Prophecy is always rash, but is more so as regards effects of the first and third kinds than as regards those which depend upon a change of imaginative outlook. I shall, therefore, speak first and chiefly about effects of this kind.

A few words about other periods of history may help to give the atmosphere. In the Middle Ages, every political question was determined by theological arguments, which took the form of analogies. The dominant controversy was between the Pope and the Emperor: it became recognised that the Pope was the Sun and the Emperor was the Moon, so the Pope won. It would be a mistake to argue that the Pope won because he had better armies; he owed his armies to the persuasive power of the Sun-and-Moon analogy, as set forth by Franciscan friars acting as recruiting sergeants. This is the kind of thing that really moves masses of men and decides important events. In the present age, some people think society is a machine and some think it is a tree. The former are Fascisti, imperialists, industrialists, Bolsheviks; the latter constitutionalists, agrarians or pacifists. The argument is just as absurd as that of the Guelfs and Ghibellines, since society is in fact neither a machine nor a tree.

With the Renaissance, we come to a new influence, the influence of literature, especially classical literature. This continues to our own day, more particularly among those who go to the public schools and the older universities. When Professor Gilbert Murray has to make up his mind on a political question, one feels that his first reaction is to ask himself, 'What would Euripides have said about it?' But this outlook is no longer dominant in the world. It was dominant in the Renaissance, and in the eighteenth century, down to and including the French Revolution. Revolutionary orators constantly appealed to shining examples of Roman virtue, and liked to conceive themselves in togas. Writers such as Montesquieu and Rousseau had an influence far surpassing what any writer can have now. One may say that the American Constitution is what Montesquieu imagined the British Constitution to be. I am not enough of a jurist to trace the influence which admiration of Rome exercised upon the Code Napoléon.

With the industrial revolution, we pass to a new era – the era of physics. Men of science, especially Galileo and Newton, had prepared the way for this era, but what brought it to birth was the embodiment of science in economic technique. A machine is a very peculiar object: it works according to known scientific laws (otherwise it would not be constructed) for a definite purpose lying outside itself, and having to do with man, usually with man's physical life. Its relation to man is exactly that which the world had to God in the Calvinist theology; perhaps that is why industrialism was invented by Protestants, and by Nonconformists rather than Anglicans. The machine-analogy has had a profound effect upon our thought. We speak of a 'mechanical' view of the world, a 'mechanical' explanation, and so on, meaning, nominally, an explanation in terms of physical laws, but introducing, perhaps unconsciously, the teleological aspect of a machine, namely, its devotion to an end outside itself. So, if society is a machine, we think that it has a purpose of an external sort. We are no longer content to say that it exists for the glory of God, but it is easy to find synonyms for God, such as: the Bank of England, the British Empire, the Standard Oil Company, the Communist Party, etc. Our wars are conflicts between these synonyms – it is the mediaeval sun-and-moon business over again.

The power of physics has been due to the fact that it is a very definite science, which has profoundly altered daily life. But this alteration has proceeded by operating on the environment, not on man himself. Given a science equally definite, and capable of altering man directly, physics would be put in the shade. This is what psychology may become. Until recent times, psychology was unimportant philosophical verbiage – the academic stuff that I learnt in youth was not worth learning. But now there are two ways of approaching psychology which are obviously important: one that of the physiologists, the other that of psycho-analysis. As the results in these two directions become more definite and more certain, it is clear that psychology will increasingly dominate men's outlook.

Let us take Education as a case in point. In old days, the received view was that education should begin at about eight years old, with the learning of Latin declensions; what happened before that was regarded as unimportant. This view, in essence, seems to be still dominant in the Labour Party, which, when in office, took much more interest in improving education after fourteen than in providing nursery schools for infants. With concentration on late education there goes a certain pessimism as to its powers: it is thought that all it can really do is to fit a man for earning a living. But one finds that the scientific tendency is to attribute more power to education than was formerly done, only it must begin very early. Psycho-analysts would begin at birth; biologists would begin even sooner. You can educate a fish to have one eye in the middle instead of two eyes, one on either side (Jennings, *Prometheus*, p. 60). But to do this you have to begin long before the fish is born. So far, there are difficulties in the way of pre-natal mammalian education, but probably they will be overcome.

But, you will say, you are using 'education' in a very funny sense. What is there in common between distorting a fish and teaching a boy Latin Grammar? I must say they seem to me very similar: both are wanton injuries inflicted for the pleasure of the experimenter. However, this would perhaps hardly do as a definition of education. The essence of education is that it is a change (other than death) effected in an organism to satisfy the desires of the operator. Of course the operator says that his desire is to improve the pupil, but this statement does not represent any objectively verifiable fact.

Now there are many ways of altering an organism. You may change its anatomy, as in the fish that has lost an eye, or the man that has lost an appendix. You may alter its metabolism, for instance by drugs. You may alter its habits by creating associations. Ordinary instruction is a particular case of this last. Now everything in education, with the exception of instruction, is easier when the organism is very young, because then it is malleable. In human beings, the important time for education is from conception to the end of the fourth year. But, as I said before, prenatal education is not yet possible, though it probably will be before the end of this century.

There are two principal methods of early education: one is by chemicals, the other by suggestion. When I say 'chemicals', perhaps I shall be thought unduly materialistic. But no one would have thought so if I had said, 'Of course a careful mother will provide the infant with the most wholesome diet available,' which is only a longer way of saying the same thing. However, I am concerned with possibilities that are more or less sensational. It may be found that the addition of suitable drugs to the diet, or the injection of the right substances into the blood, will increase intelligence or alter the emotional nature. Every one knows of the connection of idiocy with lack of iodine. Perhaps we shall find that intelligent men are those who, in infancy, got small quantities of some rare compound accidentally in their diet, owing to lack of cleanliness in the pots and pans. Or perhaps the mother's diet during pregnancy will turn out to be the decisive factor. I know nothing about this whole subject; I merely observe that we know much more about the education of salamanders than about that of human beings, chiefly because we do not imagine that salamanders have souls.

The psychological side of early education cannot well begin before birth, because it is chiefly concerned with habit-formation, and habits acquired before birth are useless afterwards, for the most part. But I think there is no doubt of the enormous influence of the early years in forming character. There is a certain opposition, to my mind quite unnecessary, between those who believe in dealing with the mind through the body, and those who believe in dealing with it directly. The old-fashioned medical man, though an earnest Christian, tends to be a materialist; he thinks that mental states have physical causes, and should be cured by removing those causes. The psycho-analyst, on the contrary, always seeks for psychological causes and tries to operate upon them. This whole thing hangs together with the mind-and-matter dualism, which I regard as a mistake. Sometimes it is easier to discover the sort of antecedent we call physical; sometimes the sort we call psychological is easier to discover. But I should suppose that both always exist, and that it is rational to operate through the one most easily discoverable in the particular case. There is no inconsistency in treating one case by administering iodine, and another by curing a phobia.

When we try to take a psychological view of politics, it is natural to begin by looking for the fundamental impulses of ordinary human beings, and the ways in which they can be developed by the environment. The orthodox economists of a hundred years ago thought that acquisitiveness was the only motive the politician need take account of; this view was adopted by Marx, and formed the basis of his economic interpretation of history. It derives naturally from physics and industrialism: it is the outcome of the imaginative domination of physics in our time. It is now held by capitalists and communists, and by all respectable persons; such as *The Times* and the magistrates, both of whom express utter amazement when young women sacrifice their earnings to marry men on the dole. The received view is that happiness is proportional to income, and that a rich old maid must be happier than a poor married woman. In order to make this true, we do all we can to inflict misery upon the latter.

As against orthodoxy and Marxianism, the psycho-analysts say that the one fundamental human impulse is sex. Acquisitiveness, they say, is a morbid development of a certain sexual perversion. It is obvious that people who believe this will act quite differently from people who take the economic view. Everybody except certain pathological cases wishes to be happy, but most people accept some current theory as to what constitutes happiness. If people think wealth constitutes happiness, they will not act as they will if they think sex the essential thing. I do not think either view quite true, but I certainly think the latter the less harmful. What does emerge is the importance of a right theory as to what constitutes happiness. In such important acts as choosing a career, a man is greatly influenced by theory. If a wrong theory prevails, successful men will be unhappy, but will not know why. This fills them with rage, which leads them to desire the slaughter of younger men, whom they envy unconsciously. Most modern politics, while nominally based on economics, is really due to rage caused by lack of instinctive satisfaction; and this lack, in turn, is largely due to false popular psychology.

I do not think that sex covers the ground. In politics, especially, sex is chiefly important when thwarted. In the war, elderly spinsters developed a ferocity partly attributable to their indignation with young men for having neglected them. They are still abnormally bellicose. I remember soon after the Armistice crossing Saltash Bridge in the train, and seeing many battleships anchored below. Two elderly spinsters in the carriage turned to each other and murmured: 'Isn't it sad to see them all lying idle!' But sex satisfied ceases to influence politics much. I should say that both hunger and thirst count for more politically. Parenthood is immensely important, because of the importance of the family; Rivers even suggested that it is the source of private property. But parenthood must not be confounded with sex.

In addition to the impulses which serve for the preservation and propagation of life, there are others concerned with what may be called Glory: love of power, vanity and rivalry. These obviously play a very great part in politics. If politics is ever to allow of a tolerable life, these glory-impulses must be tamed and taught to take no more than their proper place.

Our fundamental impulses are neither good nor bad: they are ethically neutral. Education should aim at making them take forms that are good. The old method, still beloved by Christians, was to thwart instinct; the new method is to train it. Take love of power: it is useless to preach Christian humility, which merely makes the impulse take hypocritical forms. What you have to do is to provide beneficent outlets for it. The original native impulse can be satisfied in a thousand ways – oppression, politics, business, art, science, all satisfy it when successfully practised. A man will choose the outlet for his love of power that corresponds with his skill; according to the type of skill given him in youth, he will choose one occupation or another. The purpose of our public schools is to teach the technique of oppression and no other; consequently they produce men who take up the white man's burden. But if these men could do science, many of them might prefer it. Of two activities which a man has mastered, he will generally prefer the more difficult: no chess-player will play draughts. In this way, skill may be made to minister to virtue.

As another illustration, take Fear. Rivers enumerates four kinds of reaction to danger, each appropriate in certain circumstances:

I Fear and Flight.
II Rage and Fight.
III Manipulative activity.
IV Paralysis.

It is obvious that the third is the best, but it requires the appropriate type of skill. The second is the one praised by militarists, schoolmasters, bishops, etc., under the name of 'courage'. Every governing class aims at producing it in its own members, and producing fear and flight in the subject population. So women were, until our own times, carefully trained to be timorous. And one finds still in Labour an inferiority complex, taking the form of snobbery and social submissiveness.

It is greatly to be feared that psychology will place new weapons in the hands of the holders of power. They will be able to train timidity and docility, and make the mass of men more and more like domestic animals. When I speak of the holders of power, I do not mean only the capitalists – I include all officials, even those of trade unions and Labour Parties. Every official, every man in a position of authority, wants his followers to be tame: he is indignant if they insist on having their own ideas as to what constitutes their happiness, instead of being grateful for what he is good enough to provide. In the past, the hereditary principle ensured that many of the governing class should be lazy and incompetent, which gave the others a chance. But if the governing class is to be recruited from the most energetic in each generation, who are to rise by their own efforts, the outlook for ordinary mortals is very black. It is hard to see how, in such a world, anybody can champion the rights of the lazy, i.e. of those who do not want to interfere with other people. It seems that quiet people will have to learn fearlessness and energy in youth if they are to have any chance in a world where all power is the reward of hustling. Perhaps democracy is a passing phase; if so, psychology will serve to rivet the chains on the serfs. This makes it important to secure democracy before the technique of oppression has been perfected.

Reverting to the threefold effects of a science which I enumerated at the beginning, it is clear that we cannot guess what use the holders of power will make of psychology, until we know what sort of government we are to have. Psychology, like every other science, will place new weapons in the hands of the authorities, notably the weapons of education and propaganda, both of which may, by a more finished psychological technique, be brought to the point where they will be practically irresistible. If the holders of power desire peace, they will be able to produce a pacific population; if war, a bellicose population. If they desire to generate intelligence, they will get it; if stupidity, they will get that. On this head, therefore, prophecy is quite impossible.

As to the effect of psychology upon the imagination, that will probably be of two opposite kinds. On the one hand, there will be a wider acceptance of determinism. Most men now feel uncomfortable about prayers for rain, because of meteorology; but they are not so uncomfortable about prayers for a good heart. If the causes of a good heart were as well known as the causes of rain, this difference would cease. A man who prayed for a good heart instead of calling in the doctor to rid him of bad desires would be branded as a hypocrite, if everybody could become a saint by paying a few guineas to a Harley Street specialist. With the increase of determinism would go, probably, a lessening of effort and a general increase of moral laziness – not that such an effect would be logical. I cannot say whether this would be a gain or a loss, as I do not know whether more good or harm comes from moral effort combined with faulty psychology. On the other hand, there would be an emancipation from materialism, both metaphysical and ethical; emotions would be thought more important if they formed the subject-matter of a generally recognised and practically efficacious science. This effect, I think, would be wholly good, since it would remove the erroneous notions now prevalent as to what constitutes happiness.

As to the possible effect of psychology in altering our manner of life through discoveries and inventions, I do not venture upon any forecast, as I cannot see any reason for expecting one sort of effect rather than another. For example: it may be that the most important effect will be to teach negroes to fight as well as white men, without acquiring any other new merits. Or, conversely, psychology may be used to induce negroes to practise birth control. These two possibilities would produce very different worlds, and there is no way of guessing whether one or the other or neither will be realised.

Finally: the great practical importance of psychology will come in giving ordinary men and women a more just conception of what constitutes human happiness. If people were genuinely happy, they would not be filled with envy, rage, and destructiveness. Apart from the necessaries of life, freedom for sex and parenthood is what is most needed – at least as much in the middle class as among wage-earners. It would be easy, with our present knowledge, to make instinctive happiness almost universal, if we were not thwarted by the malevolent passions of those who have missed happiness and do not want anyone else to get it. And if happiness were common, it would preserve itself, because appeals to hatred and fear, which now constitute almost the whole of politics, would fall flat. But if psychological knowledge is wielded by an aristocracy, it will prolong and intensify all the old evils. The world is full of knowledge of all sorts that might bring such happiness as has never existed since man first emerged, but old maladjustments, greed, envy and religious cruelty, stand in the way. I do not know what the outcome will be, but I think it will be either better or worse than anything the human race has yet known.

Chapter 16

The Danger of Creed Wars

Various periodic oscillations run through the history of mankind, and any one of them may be regarded by an enthusiastic person as the key to history. The one with which I propose to deal is perhaps not the least important; it is the oscillation from synthesis and intolerance to analysis and tolerance, and back again.

Uncivilised tribes are almost always synthetic and intolerant: there must be no departure from social customs, and strangers are viewed with the gravest suspicion. The pre-Hellenic civilisations of historical times on the whole retained these characteristics; in Egypt, more especially, the powerful priesthood was the guardian of the national traditions, and was able to repel the solvent scepticism which Akhnaton acquired from contact with the alien civilisation of Syria. Whatever may have been the case in the Minoan period, the first full historical age of analytic tolerance was that of Greece. The cause, then as in subsequent instances, was commerce, with its experience of foreigners and its need of friendly relations with them. Commerce was, until very recent years, a matter of individual enterprise, in which prejudices were a hindrance to profits, and *laissez-faire* was the rule of success. But in Greece, as in later times, the commercial spirit, while it inspired art and thought, could not produce the degree of social cohesion required for military success. The Greeks therefore succumbed first to Macedonia and then to Rome.

The Roman system was essentially synthetic, and intolerant in a quite modern way, i.e. not theologically, but imperialistically and financially. The Roman synthesis, however, was slowly dissolved by Greek scepticism, and gave place to the Christian and Mohammedan syntheses, which dominated the world until the Renaissance. In Western Europe the Renaissance produced a brief period of intellectual and artistic splendour, leading to political chaos and the determination of plain men to have done with this fooling and revert to the serious business of killing each other in the wars of religion. The commercial nations, Holland and England, were the first to emerge from the intolerance of the Reformation and Counter-Reformation, and showed their tolerance by fighting each other instead of combining against the adherents of Rome. England, like ancient Greece, has had a solvent effect upon neighbours, and has gradually produced the degree of scepticism required for democracy and parliamentary government, which are scarcely possible in an intolerant age, and are therefore tending to be replaced by Fascism and Bolshevism.

The world of the nineteenth century, more than is generally realised, is due to the philosophy embodied in the revolution of 1688 and expressed by John Locke. This philosophy dominated America in 1776 and France in 1789, spreading thence to the rest of the Western world, largely as a result of the prestige which England acquired through the industrial revolution and the defeat of Napoleon.

It is only quite gradually that men have become aware of an essential inconsistency in this situation. The ideas of Locke and of nineteenth-century Liberalism were commercial, not industrial: the philosophy appropriate to industrialism is quite different from that of seafaring merchant adventurers. Industrialism is synthetic; it builds up large economic units, makes society more organic, and demands a suppression of individualistic impulses. Moreover, the economic organisation of industrialism has hitherto been oligarchic, and has neutralised political democracy in the very moment of its apparent victory. For these reasons it seems likely that we are entering upon a new age of synthetic intolerance, involving, as such ages always do, wars between rival philosophies or creeds. It is this probability that I wish to explore.

There are in the world today only two great Powers: one is the United States, the other is the USSR. Their populations are about equal; so are the populations of the other nations which they dominate. The United States dominates the rest of the American continent and Western Europe; the USSR dominates Turkey, Persia, and most of China. The division is reminiscent of the mediaeval division between Christian and Mussulman; there is the same kind of difference of creed, the same implacable hostility, and a similar though more extended division of territory.

Just as there were in the Middle Ages wars between Christian Powers and wars between Mohammedan Powers, so there will be wars within these two great groups; but we may expect that they will be terminated, sooner or later, by genuine peace treaties, whereas between the two great groups there will only be truces produced by mutual exhaustion. I do not suppose that either group can be victorious, or can derive any advantage from the conflict; I suppose the conflict maintained because each group hates the other and regards it as wicked. This is a characteristic of creed wars.

I am not, of course, suggesting that a development of this sort is *sure* to come about: in human affairs the future must always be uncertain until science has advanced very much further than it has done yet. I suggest only that there are potent forces tending in the direction indicated. Since these forces are psychological, they are within human control; therefore if a future of creed wars seems disagreeable to the holders of power, they can avert it. In making any unpleasant prophecy about the future, provided the prophecy is not based upon purely physical considerations, part of the object of the prophet is to induce people to make the efforts necessary to falsify his predictions. The prophet of evil, if he is a philanthropist, should therefore seek to make himself hated, and let it seem as though he would be much vexed if events failed to confirm his forecast. With this preliminary, I propose to examine the grounds for expecting creed wars, and afterward the measures that will be necessary if they are to be averted.

The fundamental reason for expecting a greater degree of effective intolerance in the near future than in the eighteenth and nineteenth centuries is the cheapness of large-scale standard production. The result of this in leading to trusts and monopolies is an ancient commonplace, as old, at least, as the Communist Manifesto. But it is the consequences in the intellectual sphere that concern us in the present connection. There is an increasing tendency for control of the sources of opinion to become concentrated in a few hands, with the result that minority opinions lose the chance of effective expression. In the USSR this concentration has been carried out deliberately and politically in the interests of the dominant party. At first it seemed very doubtful whether such a method could succeed, but as the years pass success becomes more and more probable. Concessions have been made in economic practice, but not in economic or political theory, nor yet in philosophical outlook. Communism is becoming more and more a creed, concerned with a future heaven, and less and less a way of life for this mundane existence. A new generation is growing up which takes this creed for granted, having never heard it effectively questioned during the formative years. If the present control over literature, the Press and education lasts for another twenty years – and there is no reason to suppose that it will not – the communist philosophy will be the one accepted by the immense majority of vigorous men. It will be combated, on the one hand, by a diminishing remnant of elderly discontented men, out of touch with affairs and with the main stream of the national life; on the other hand by a few free-thinkers, whose influence is likely to remain negligible for a long time. There have always been free-thinkers – the Italian aristocracy in the thirteenth century were largely Epicureans – but they have only been important when, owing to some accidental circumstance, their opinions were useful to important groups for economic or political reasons, as at the present moment in Mexico. This can always be avoided by a little good sense on the part of the Established Church, and one may assume that this modicum of good sense will be displayed by the Established Church in Russia. With the spread of education, the young peasants are being brought into the fold, and their conversion to the theory is facilitated by the increasing concessions to the individualism of peasant practice. The less Communism there is in the actual economic régime, the more there will be in the generally accepted creed.

Nor is it only in Russia, or in the territories of the USSR, that this process is taking place. In China it is beginning, and may not improbably become very strong. Whatever is vigorous in China – more particularly the Nationalist Government – began under Russian influence. Military successes won by the Southern armies have been largely due to propaganda organised under Russian guidance. Those Chinese who cling to the ancient religions – Buddhism and Taoism – are politically reactionary; the Christians tend to be more friendly to foreigners than is pleasing to the nationalists. In the main, the nationalists are opposed to all old religions, whether native or foreign. The new religion of Russia attracts the patriotic intelligentsia, both as being the latest thing, the last word in 'progress', and also because it is associated with a politically friendly Power, in fact the only friendly Power. While, therefore, it is impossible to imagine China instituting Communism in *practice*, it is quite probable that it may adopt the *philosophy* of the Bolsheviks.

One of the great mistakes of the British in their dealings with 'backward' nations has been their excessive belief in the power of tradition. You will find in China many Englishmen with a considerable knowledge of the Chinese classics, with an understanding of popular superstitions, and with friends among the older Conservative *literati*. You will find hardly any who understand Young China, or view it with anything but ignorant contempt. In the face of the transformation of Japan, they continue to judge China's future by her past, and to assume that no great rapid change is possible. I am convinced that this is an illusion. As in Japan, so in China, the military and economic strength of the West has given it prestige and at the same time caused it to be hated. But for Russia, the hatred might remain impotent; as it is, Russia offers a model in emancipation from the West and help to the Chinese in travelling a more or less similar road. In these circumstances rapid change is very possible. Rapid change is always easier to effect in dealing with a hitherto uneducated population, because education backed by the prestige of government can easily cause the young to despise their illiterate elders.

It is therefore by no means improbable that, twenty years hence, the Bolshevik ideology will be in power throughout China, and will be combined with a close political alliance with Russia. Gradually, by means of education, this ideology will be instilled into about half the population of the globe. What, meanwhile, will happen to the other half?

In the Western world, where official orthodoxy has the advantage of the *status quo* and tradition, more subtle methods suffice; indeed, the methods which exist have largely grown up without set purpose. The modern creed is not seen in its purity in Europe, where remnants of the Middle Ages interfere. It is in the United States that industrial capitalism has the freest hand, and that its character is most obvious. But Western Europe must, bit by bit, take on the American character, in view of the fact that America is the greatest of World Powers. I do not mean that we shall have to adopt fundamentalism, for example, which is merely a belated European creed surviving among a transplanted population of pious peasants. The agricultural portion of America is not the internationally important part, nor the part whose outlook is likely to shape the future of America. It is the industrial creed that is important and novel. This creed has one form in Russia, and another in America; the contrast of these two forms is what concerns the world.

America, like Russia, has an ideal which is not realised, but to which values are theoretically adjusted. The Russian ideal is Communism. The American ideal is free competition. What the New Economic Policy was as a stumbling-block to the Russian ideal, trusts are to the American ideal. Where the communist thinks in terms of organisations, the typical American thinks in terms of individuals. *From Log Cabin to White House* represents the ideal to be put before the young in politics, and a similar ideal in the economic sphere inspires the advertisements of systems for securing business advancement. The fact that it is impossible for everyone to occupy the White House or become President of a corporation is not held to be a defect in the ideal, but only a reason for urging every young man to be more industrious and cunning than his fellows. While America was still empty it was possible for most people to achieve a considerable measure of success without standing upon the shoulders of the others; even now, so long as a man cares only for material prosperity, not for power, a wage-earner in America can be richer than a professional man on the Continent.

But power is becoming concentrated, and there is a danger lest those who are excluded should come to demand their share. A part of the national creed is designed to minimise this danger. The Napoleonic maxim of *La carrière ouverte aux talents* does a great deal; the rest is done by representing success as an individual rather than a collective affair. In the communist philosophy the success which is sought is that of a group or an organisation; in the American philosophy it is that of an individual. Consequently the individual who fails feels ashamed of his incapacity rather than angry with the social system. And the individualist philosophy to which he is accustomed prevents him from imagining that there is anything to be gained by collective action. There is therefore no effective opposition to the holders of power, who remain free to enjoy the advantages of a social system which gives them wealth and world-wide influence.

There never has been a period when the things that men desire were evenly distributed throughout the population. In a stable social system there must be some method of making the less fortunate acquiesce in their lot, and this is usually some kind of creed. But in order to secure widespread acceptance, a creed has to offer advantages to the whole community sufficiently great to compensate for the injustices which it condones. In America it offers technical progress and increase in the general standard of material comfort. It may not be able to go on providing the latter indefinitely, but probably it will do so for some time to come. In Russia it offers the conception of industry conducted for the benefit of all, not only of the capitalists. No doubt the Russian wage-earner is poorer than the American, but he has the consolation of knowing (or at least believing) that he is receiving his fair share, and is not suffering unnecessarily to make someone else great and grand. Moreover, he feels himself a unit in a closely-knit co-operative community, not one of a mass of units all struggling one against the other.

I think we come here to the kernel of the difference between the creeds of America and Russia. America, whose outlook is moulded by the Protestant tradition and a century of pioneering, believes in the individual fighting his way by his unaided efforts from poverty to affluence. In imagination he is supposed to be fighting the wilderness like the backwoodsman; if in fact it is against human competitors that he fights, that is not a matter upon which it is necessary to dwell. Nor is it good form to stress the fact that he will be probably all his life a slave as regards the expression of opinion, winning material comfort by the sacrifice of mental integrity. The opinions which he must not express are obviously undesirable opinions, and to compel him to hold his tongue about them is only to exercise a wholesome restraint upon anarchic impulses. By the time he is middle-aged he himself is in complete agreement with this point of view.

In Russia, on the contrary, the Byzantine Church, the Tartars, and the Tsardom have successively impressed upon the popular mind the nothingness of the individual; what he formerly sacrificed to God or the Tsar can be sacrificed with less difficulty to the community. Russian Communists differ from their sympathisers in the West chiefly in this matter of lack of respect for the individual. (See René Fülöp-Miller, *Giest und Gesicht der*

Bolschewismus.) In this they can be more thorough than their Byzantine predecessors, who believed in the soul and the prospect of immortality. Having abolished the soul, the rulers of the USSR can accept the analogy of Leviathan more whole-heartedly than is possible for a Christian. To them the individualism of the West is as absurd as if the separate parts of the human body were to set up to live for themselves as in the fable of Menenius Agrippa. This is the root of their views on art, on religion, on ethics, on the family – indeed, on everything.

Socialists in the West sometimes speak as if they held similar views as to the paramount importance of the community, but in fact they seldom do. They would think it natural, for example, that a man who migrates to a distant place should wish to take his wife and children with him, but to the more thoroughgoing Eastern communists this would seem mere sentimentalism. They would say that his children could be cared for by the State, and he could no doubt get a new wife, just as good as the old one, in the place to which he was going. The claims of natural affection would be thought a trivial matter. It is true that similar things are tolerated in the practice of capitalist societies, but not to the same extent in their theories. It is true also that the cult of Lenin runs counter to what I have been saying. This, I think, must be admitted to be an inconsistency, an eruption of the natural man through the crust of theory. But I fancy a full-fledged communist would say that Lenin is revered as the incarnation of a Force rather than as a concrete individual. He may in time become as theoretically abstract as the Logos.

There have been some who have supposed that the Russian philosophy would suddenly or gradually conquer the West. In favour of this view there are certain considerations that might at first sight seem to carry great weight. Undoubtedly the communist philosophy is more suited to industrialism than the philosophy of capitalism, because industrialism inevitably increases the importance of organisations as against individuals, and also because individual ownership of land and natural resources belongs more naturally to an agricultural than to an industrial régime. There have been two sources of private ownership of land: the one aristocratic, based everywhere upon the right of the sword, the other democratic, based upon the right of the peasant to own the land which he cultivates himself. Both these rights become illogical and absurd in an industrial community. Mining royalties and urban landlordism exhibit the absurdity of the aristocratic form of land-ownership, since it cannot be pretended that the revenue derived by the owner has any social utility. But the right of the peasant to the land which he cultivates may lead to equal absurdities. A Boer farmer on whose farm gold is found acquires wealth to which he is in no way entitled by any service which he performs to the community. So does the man who has a farm in a district which becomes urban. Not only private ownership, but even national ownership may easily involve absurdities. It would be ridiculous to pretend that Egypt and the Republic of Panama should control the canals in their territories, and nothing but harm comes of the notion that undeveloped countries have an indefeasible right to the control of such things as oil which may be found upon their territories. The theoretical argument for the international control of raw materials is irresistible, and only the agricultural tradition leads us to tolerate the fact that wealthy highwaymen are allowed to levy toll upon the world for the use of indispensable minerals.

Industrial communities are much more closely knit than agricultural communities, and legal powers which can be accorded to individuals without great harm in the latter become extremely dangerous in the former. Moreover, there is the obvious appeal to envy (otherwise known as a sense of justice), which works on the side of the socialist. But in spite of these considerations I do not think that the socialistic outlook is likely to become common in America at any time during the next hundred years, and unless America is socialistic in opinion, no nation within its economic orbit will be allowed to practise even a modicum of Socialism, as was seen by the abolition of the State ownership of railways in Germany under the Dawes Scheme.

My reasons for saying that America will not become socialistic are based upon the belief that American prosperity will continue. So long as the American working-man is richer than the working-man in a socialist country, it will be possible for capitalistic propaganda to rebut the arguments in favour of economic change. In this respect the economies of large-scale production which I mentioned earlier are of paramount importance. Syndicated newspapers, higher education subsidised by millionaires, elementary education controlled by the Churches, which in turn profit by the donations of millionaires, a well-organised book-trade, which can decide by advertisement which books shall sell widely, and can produce them much more cheaply than books with a limited circulation, radio, but, above all, the cinema, where immensely expensive productions are made to pay by being exhibited throughout the Western world – all these things make for uniformity, for centralised control of ideas and news, for the dissemination of only such creeds and philosophies as are approved by the holders of power.

I do not think that such propaganda is wholly and inevitably irresistible, but I do think it is likely to prevail so long as the régime which it recommends appears to the common man to bear the marks of success. Defeat in war, which is a mark of failure that everybody can understand, may upset any régime, but the prospect of America being defeated in war is remote. One may therefore expect the same kind of popular enthusiasm for the American system in America as there was in England for parliamentary government in the nineteenth century when England was successful. Of course, differences in economic creeds between East and West will continue to be reinforced by differences of theology in the old-fashioned sense. One may expect America to remain Christian and the East anti-Christian. One may expect America to continue to pay lip-service to Christian doctrines of marriage and the family, while the East regards these as outworn superstitions. One may expect that on both sides there will be cruelty on a large scale, and that propaganda will cause each side to know the cruelties of the other, but not its own. Very few Americans, for example, know the truth about Sacco and Vanzetti: condemned to death for a murder to which another man confessed, and the evidence for which has been acknowledged by policemen engaged in collecting it to have been a 'frame-up'. A new trial was refused to these men partly on the ground that the man who confessed to the murder was a bad character. Apparently, in the opinion of American judges, only persons of good character commit murders. The real crime of Sacco and Vanzetti was that they were anarchists. All these facts are, of course, known in Russia, where they tend to produce an unfavourable opinion as to capitalistic justice. Similarly, the Russian trials of Patriarchs and Social Revolutionaries are known in America. Thus each side acquires abundant evidence to prove the other wicked, but remains ignorant of its own wickedness.

I met recently a professor in the University of California who had never heard of Mooney, imprisoned in a Californian gaol for a murder he is known to have probably not committed, in spite of the fact that during the Kerensky régime the Russian Government made official representatives to the Government of the United States about this case, and President Wilson appointed a commission to inquire into it, which reported that there was no good ground for supposing him guilty. But he is a communist.

Persecution for opinion is thus tolerated in all countries. In Switzerland it is not only legal to murder a communist, but the man who has done so is exonerated for his next crime on the ground that he is a first offender. This state of affairs causes no indignation outside the Soviet Republic. The best of the capitalist countries in this respect is Japan, where the policeman who strangled two eminent anarchists and their little nephew (whom he mistook for their son) in a police-station was sentenced to a term of imprisonment, in spite of the fact that he had become a popular hero and that school-children were invited to write themes in his praise.

For these reasons I do not think it likely that any country in which the existing régime appears to the common man to be successful, or in which American economic influence is uppermost, will adopt the communistic creed within any measurable future. On the contrary, it seems probable that the defence of the *status quo* will lead the holders of power to become increasingly conservative and to support all such conservative forces as they find in the community. The strongest of these, of course, is religion. In the plebiscite in Germany about royal property the Churches ruled officially that it would be anti-Christian to confiscate any of it. Such opinions deserve to be rewarded. They no doubt will be.

I think it is to be expected that organised religion, and more particularly the Catholic Church, will become increasingly powerful in all capitalist countries as a result of a tighter control over education in the interests of the rich. The opposition between Russia and the West, therefore, though fundamentally economic, may be expected to extend over the whole sphere of belief. When I speak of belief I mean dogmatic opinions on matters as to which the truth is not known. The whole evil could, of course, be avoided by the spread of the scientific spirit, that is to say, by the habit of forming opinions on evidence rather than on prejudice; but although scientific technique is necessary to industrialism, the scientific spirit belongs rather to commerce, since it is necessarily individualistic and uninfluenced by authority. We may therefore expect to see it surviving only in small countries, such as Holland, Denmark and Scandinavia, which lie outside the main current of modern life.

But it is not improbable that gradually, after a century or so of conflict, both sides will grow weary, as they did after the Thirty Years War. When that time comes, the latitudinarians will again have their chance.

For my part, I look upon the coming strife as Erasmus did, without the ability to join whole-heartedly with either party. No doubt I agree with the Bolsheviks on many more points than with the American magnates, but I cannot believe that their philosophy is ultimately true or capable of producing a happy world. I admit that individualism, which has been increasing ever since the Renaissance, has gone too far, and that a more co-operative spirit is necessary if industrial societies are to be stable and to bring contentment to the average man and woman. But the difficulty in the Bolshevik philosophy, as in that of America, is that the principle of organisation for them is economic, whereas the groupings that are consonant with human instinct are biological. The family and the nation are biological, the trust and the trade union are economic. The harm that is done at present by biological groupings is undeniable, but I do not think the social problem can be solved by ignoring the instincts which produce those groupings. I am convinced, for example, that if all children were educated in State institutions without the co-operation of the parents, a large proportion of men and women would lose the incentive to arduous activity and would become listless and bored. Nationalism also perhaps has its place, though clearly armies and navies are an undesirable expression of it, and its proper sphere is cultural rather than political. Human beings can be greatly changed by institutions and education, but if they are changed in such a way as to thwart fundamental instincts, the result is a loss of vigour. And the Bolsheviks certainly are mistaken in speaking as though the economic instinct were the only one of psychological importance. They share this mistake with the competitive society of the West, although the West is less explicit in the matter.

The fundamental delusion of our time, in my opinion, is the

excessive emphasis upon the economic aspects of life, and I do not expect the strife between Capitalism and Communism as philosophies to cease until it is recognised that both are inadequate through their failure to recognise biological needs.

As to the methods of diminishing the ferocity of the struggle, I do not know of anything better than the old Liberal watchwords, yet I feel that they are likely to be very ineffective. What is needed is freedom of opinion, and opportunity for the spread of opinion. It is the latter particularly that causes the difficulty. The mechanism for the effective and widespread diffusion of an opinion must necessarily be in the hands either of the State or of great capitalistic concerns. Before the introduction of democracy and education this was much less true: effective opinion was confined to a small minority, who could be reached without all the expensive apparatus of modern propaganda. But it can hardly be expected that either the State or a great capitalist organisation will devote money and energy to the propagation of opinions which it considers dangerous and subversive, and contrary to true morality. The State, no less than the capitalist organisation, is in practice a stupid elderly man accustomed to flattery, ossified in his prejudices, and wholly unaware of all that is vital in the thought of his time. No novelty can be effectively advocated until it has passed the censorship of some such old fogy. It is true that hole-and-corner publicity is possible, but this only obtains hole-and-corner readers.

The evil is an increasing one, since the whole tendency of modern business is amalgamation and centralisation. The only method of securing wide publicity for an unpopular cause is that which was adopted by the suffragettes, and that is only suitable where the issue is simple and passionate, nor where it is intricate and argumentative. The effect of the official or unofficial censorship is therefore to make opposition to it passionate rather than rational and to render calm discussion of the evidence for or against an innovation only possible in obscure ways which never reach the general public.

For example, there is an official medical publication exposing worthless patent medicines, but no newspaper will mention it and hardly anyone knows of its existence; on the other hand, the Christian Scientists, who maintain that all medicines are equally worthless, are able to obtain publicity. Exactly analogous things happen in politics. Extreme opinions on either side can obtain publicity, while moderate and rational opinions are thought too dull to bear down the opposition of the authorities. This evil is, however, much less in England than in most other countries, because England has been predominantly commercial and has retained the love of freedom associated with commerce.

It would, of course, be possible to devise remedies if one could suppose that those in authority felt the need of them. It would be possible to educate people in such a way as to increase their powers of weighing evidence and forming rational judgements, instead of which they are taught patriotism and class bias. Perhaps in time men may come to feel that intelligence is an asset to a community, but I cannot say that I see much sign of any movement in this direction.

Chapter 17

Some Prospects: Cheerful and Otherwise

I

There are two ways of writing about the future, the scientific and the Utopian. The scientific way tries to discover what is probable; the Utopian way sets out what the writer would like. In a well-developed science such as astronomy no one would adopt the Utopian method: people do not prophesy eclipses because it would be pleasant if they took place. But in social affairs those who profess to have discovered general laws enabling them to foretell future developments are usually not so scientific as they pretend to be; there must be a great deal of guesswork in any attempt to say what is going to happen to human institutions. We do not know, for instance, what difference may be made by new discoveries. Perhaps people will find out how to go to Mars or Venus. Perhaps almost all our food will be manufactured in chemical laboratories instead of being grown in the fields. To such possibilities there is no end. I shall ignore them, and consider only tendencies which are already well developed. And I shall also assume that our civilisation will continue, although this is by no means certain. It may be destroyed by wars, or by a gradual decay such as occurred in the later Roman Empire. But if it survives, it is likely to have certain characteristics, and it is these that I shall be attempting to discover.

In addition to the introduction of machinery, and largely as a result of it, there has been another change: society has become far more organised than it was formerly. Printing, railways the telegraph, and (now) broadcasting have provided the technical means for large organisations such as a modern State or an international financial business. Public affairs play almost no part in the life of an Indian or Chinese peasant, whereas in England they are a matter of interest to almost every one even in the remotest country districts. This was not the case until recently; one would gather from Jane Austen that the country gentry of her time hardly noticed the Napoleonic wars. I should put as the most important change in modern times the tendency toward closer social organisation.

Connected with this is another result of science, namely, the greater unity of the world. Before the sixteenth century, America and the Far East were almost unrelated to Europe; since that time their relations have become continually closer. Augustus in Rome and the Han Emperor in China simultaneously imagined themselves masters of the whole civilised world; nowadays such pleasing illusions are impossible. Practically every part of the world has relations to practically every other part, which may be either friendly or hostile, but are in either case important. The Dalai Llama, after centuries of isolation, found himself courted by both Russians and British; he took refuge from their embarrassing attentions in Peking, where all his suite arrived duly armed with kodaks from America.

From these two premises, of closer social organisation and greater unity in the world, it follows that, if our civilisation is to develop, there will have to be a central authority to control the whole world. For, if not, causes of dispute will multiply and wars will become more intense owing to the growth of public spirit. The central authority may not be a formal government; I think it likely that it will not be. It is far more likely to be a combination of financiers, who have become persuaded that peace is to their interest because money lent to belligerent States is often lost. Or it may be a single dominant State (America), or a group of States (America and the British Empire). But before such a condition is reached, there may be a long period in which the world is virtually divided between America and Russia, the former controlling Western Europe and the self-governing Dominions, the latter controlling all Asia. Two such groups would be strong for defence and weak for attack, so that they might subsist for a century or more. Ultimately, however – I mean at latest some time during the twenty-first century – there must be either a cataclysm or a central authority controlling the whole world. I shall assume that civilised mankind will have enough sense, or that America will have enough power, to prevent a cataclysm involving a return to barbarism. If so, what powers must the central authority possess?

First and foremost, it must be able to decide questions of peace and war, or to ensure that if there is war the side which it favours wins a speedy victory. This end may be secured by financial supremacy alone, without formal political control. As war becomes more scientific it becomes more expensive, so that the leading financiers of the world, if they combined, could decide the issue by giving or withholding loans. And by the sort of pressure which has been brought to bear upon Germany since the Treaty of Versailles they could secure the virtual disarmament of any group that they dislike. In this way they would gradually come to control all the large armed forces of the world. This is the fundamental condition for the other activities which they would have to undertake.

In addition to revising treaties and intervening in disputes, there are three matters which would have to be decided by the central authority. They are (1) the allocation of territory to the different national States, (2) movements of population across the boundaries of national States, and (3) the rationing of raw materials as between different claimants. Each of these demands a few words.

(1) Questions of territorial allegiance are treated at present with an absurd solemnity which has grown out of the old personal allegiance to a sovereign. If a person in one State gives expression to the opinion that the district in which he lives ought to belong to another State he is guilty of treason, and liable to severe punishment. And yet, in itself, his opinion is as much a legitimate matter of political debate as any other. We do not feel any horror of a citizen of (say) Croydon who holds that Croydon ought to count as part of London. But a citizen of Colombia who holds that his village should belong to Venezuela is regarded by his Government as a monster of iniquity. The central authority will have to prevent the national governments from acting upon such prejudices, and will have to treat territorial readjustments rationally, i.e. mainly by the wishes of the local population, but also in part by economic and cultural considerations.

(2) Movements of population are likely to raise increasingly difficult problems as years go by. It is natural for population to flow from places where wages are low to those where they are high. This is now permitted within a single country, but not throughout a super-national federation such as the British Empire. Asiatic immigration is almost totally prohibited in America and

the self-governing Dominions, and European immigration into America is becoming more and more restricted. The forces on both sides in this matter are immensely powerful. They afford a stimulus to Asiatic militarism, and may ultimately cause it to become so strong that it can challenge the white race – say during the next great war between white nations.

Ultimately, if war on a large scale has been eliminated and public health has been immensely improved by medicine and hygiene, it will become essential to the preservation of peace and well-being that the backward nations shall limit the increase of population, as the more civilised nations are already doing. Those who in principle oppose birth control are either incapable of arithmetic or else in favour of war, pestilence and famine as permanent features of human life. One may assume that the international authority will insist upon freedom to limit births among backward races and classes, and will not, as governments do now, insist that only the intelligent shall have small families.

(3) The last matter, the rationing of raw material, is perhaps the most important of all. Wars are likely to be very largely concerned with raw material; it is notorious what a large part oil, coal and iron have played in post-war disputes. I am not assuming that raw materials will be rationed justly, but merely that they will be rationed in some way by an authority having irresistible force at its command. I believe that the problem of organising the world as a single economic and political unit will have to be solved before questions of justice can be tackled successfully. I am an international socialist, but I expect to see internationalism realised sooner than Socialism.

II

Assuming that within the next one hundred and fifty years a central authority is developed, strong enough to reduce all wars to the level of sporadic revolts quickly suppressed, what kind of economic changes are likely to be associated with this development? Will the general level of well-being be increased? Will competition survive, or will production be monopolistic? In the latter case, will the monopolies be in private hands or in those of the

State? And will the products of labour be distributed with less injustice than at present?

There are here two different kinds of questions: one is concerned with the forms of economic organisation, the other with the principles of distribution. The latter will depend upon political power: every class and every nation always secures as great a share of wealth as it can, and it is ultimately armed force that decides how large this share shall be. Let us first discuss organisation, and leave distribution alone for the moment.

A study of history reveals a somewhat humiliating fact about organisation. Whenever an increase in the size of organisations has been desirable in the interests of those concerned, it has had to be brought about (with negligible exceptions) by means of force on the part of the stronger. Where voluntary federation was the only available method no unity has been achieved. It was so with ancient Greece in the face of Macedonia, with sixteenth-century Italy in the face of France and Spain, with present-day Europe in the face of America and Asia. I assume, therefore, that the central authority will be brought into being by force, or the threat of force, not by a voluntary organisation such as the League of Nations, which will never be strong enough to coerce recalcitrant Great Powers. I think, also, that the power of the central authority will be primarily economic, and will rest upon possession of raw materials combined with control of financial credit. I conceive of it as consisting, in the beginning, of a group of financiers backed, informally, by one or more great States.

It follows that at the basis of the economic structure there will be monopoly. All the oil supply of the world, for example, will be centrally controlled. It follows that aeroplanes and oil-driven warships will be useless to Powers which conflict with the central authority, unless they can be used to capture an oil-field by a brief raid. The same will apply to other things in less obvious ways. Already at the present day a large proportion of the world's meat supply is controlled by the Big Five in Chicago, who are themselves to some extent controlled by Messrs J. P. Morgan & Co. From the raw material to the finished commodity there is a long road to travel, and monopoly may intervene at any stage. In the case of oil the natural stage is at the beginning. In other cases, it may be harbours or ships or railways that give the monopolist his opportunity to control. But wherever he intervenes, he is stronger than any of the other parties concerned.

Given monopoly at one stage of a process there will be a tendency to extend the monopoly to earlier and later stages. The growth of economic monopoly is part of the general tendency to increase of organisation, which is shown politically in the greater power and size of States. We may therefore confidently expect a continuation of the process of eliminating competition which has been going on throughout the last half-century. It is of course to be assumed that trade unions will continue to diminish competition among wage-earners. The view that while employers are organised wage-earners should be prevented by law from counter-organising is not one which it will be found long possible to maintain.

Secure peace and adequate control of production ought to lead to a great increase of material comfort, provided it is not all swallowed up by an increase of population. Whether the world, at that stage, is capitalistic or socialistic, we may expect an improvement in the economic position of all classes. But this brings us to our second question, that of distribution.

Assuming a dominant group associated with a dominant nation (or several dominant nations in alliance), it is of course obvious that the dominant group will secure great wealth to itself, and will produce contentment in the population of the dominant nation by conceding to its wage-earners a progressive increase in their earnings. This has been happening in the United States, as it formerly happened in England. So long as there is a rapid increase in the total wealth of a nation it is easy for capitalists to prevent successful socialist propaganda by timely monetary control. And the less fortunate nations can be kept subdued by a system of imperialistic control.

But such a system will probably develop in the direction of democracy, i.e. of Socialism – for Socialism is merely economic democracy in a community which has reached the stage of monopoly in many industries. One may take the political development of England as a parallel. England was unified by the King – a process practically completed by Henry VII after the anarchy of the Wars of the Roses. The royal power was necessary to produce unity, but when unity had been achieved the movement toward democracy began almost at once, and it was found, after the troubles of the seventeenth century, that democracy was compatible with public order. We are now, in the economic sphere, just about at the transition from the Wars of the Roses to Henry VII. When once economic unity, however despotic, has been achieved, the movement toward economic democracy will be immensely strengthened, since it will no longer have to contend with the fear of anarchy. Minorities can only retain power if they have considerable support in public opinion, since they must be loyally served by their armies and navies and civil servants. Situations will continually arise in which the holders of economic power will find it prudent to make concessions; in the control of affairs they will have to associate with themselves representatives of the less fortunate nations and classes, and this process will probably continue until a completely democratic régime has been established.

Since we have been assuming a central authority which controls the whole world, democracy in regard to this authority would be international democracy, embracing not only the white races, but also the races of Asia and Africa. Asia is developing at present with such extraordinary rapidity that it may well be capable of taking a worthy part in the government of the world by the time such a government comes into existence. Africa is a more difficult problem. But even in Africa the French (who are in this respect our superiors) are achieving remarkable results, and no one can foretell what may be accomplished within the next hundred years. I conclude, therefore, that a system of world-wide Socialism, involving economic justice to all nations and classes, may well become possible not long after the establishment of a central authority. And, if so, the natural operation of political forces is pretty sure to bring it about.

There are, however, other possibilities, which might lead to a perpetuation of caste distinctions. Wherever white men and negroes live side by side, as in South Africa and the Southern States of America, it has been found possible to combine democracy for white men with a semi-servile condition for the coloured population. What stands in the way of this development on a large scale is the objection by Labour to coloured immigration in most parts of the English-speaking world. Nevertheless, it remains a possibility to be borne in mind. I shall have something more to say about it later.

III

What is likely to be the development of the family during the next two centuries? We cannot tell, but we can note certain forces at work which are likely, if unchecked, to have certain results. I wish to state, at the outset, that I am not concerned with what I desire, but with what I expect, which is a very different thing. The world has never in the past developed just as I should have wished, and I see no reason to think that it will do so in future.

There are certain things in modern civilised communities which are tending to weaken the family; the chief of them is humanitarian sentiment toward children. More and more, people come to feel that children should not suffer more than can be helped through their parents' misfortunes or even sins. In the Bible the lot of the orphan is always spoken of as very sad, and so no doubt it was; nowadays he suffers little more than other children. There will be a growing tendency for the State or charitable institutions to give fairly adequate care to neglected children, and consequently children will be more and more neglected by unconscientious parents or guardians. Gradually the expense of caring for neglected children out of public funds will become so great that there will be a very strong inducement for all who are not well off to avail themselves of the opportunities for giving their children over to the State; probably this will be done, in the end, as now with schooling, by practically all who are below a certain economic level.

The effects of such a change would be very far-reaching. With parental responsibility removed, marriage would no longer be felt important, and would gradually cease among those classes which left their children to the State. In civilised countries, the number of children produced under these conditions would probably be very small, and the State would have to fix a payment to mothers at a scale found adequate to produce the number of citizens which it considered desirable. All this is not so very remote; it might easily happen in England before the end of the twentieth century.

If all this happens while the capitalist system and the international anarchy are still in force, the results are likely to be terrible. To begin with, there will be profound division between the proletarians, who will virtually have neither parents nor children, and the well-to-do, who will preserve the family system with inheritance of property. The proletarians, being educated by the State, will be imbued, like the Janissaries in old Turkey, with a passionate militaristic loyalty. The women will be taught that it is their duty to have many children, both to keep down the tariff of State payments for children and to increase the supply of soldiers for killing the population of other countries. With no parental propaganda to counteract that of the State, there will be no limit to the anti-foreign ferocity with which children can be imbued, so that when they grow up they will fight blindly for their masters. Men whose opinions the Government dislikes will be punished by having their children confiscated to the State institutions.

It is thus quite possible that through the joint operation of patriotism and humanitarian feeling for children we may be led, step by step, to the creation of a society profoundly divided into two different castes, the upper retaining marriage and family loyalties, the lower feeling loyalty only to the State. For military reasons the State will secure, by payment, a high birth-rate among the proletarians; hygiene and medicine will secure a low death-rate. War will therefore be the only way of keeping the population of the world within limits, except starvation, which nations will try to avert by fighting. In these circumstances we may expect an era of internecine wars, comparable only to the invasions of Huns and Mongols in the Middle Ages. The only hope will lie in the speedy victory of some one nation or group of nations.

The results of State care of children will be almost diametrically opposite to the above if a world-wide authority has been previously established. In that case the central authority will not permit the children to be taught a militaristic patriotism, and will not permit the various national States to pay for an increase of population beyond what is economically desirable. The children brought up in State institutions will, if the pressure of militaristic necessities is removed, almost certainly be better developed both physically and mentally than the average child is now, and a very rapid progress will therefore become possible.

But even if a central authority exists the effects will be profoundly different if the world remains capitalistic from what they will be if it has adopted Socialism. In the former alternative there will be that division of castes which we spoke of a moment ago, the upper caste retaining the family, the lower substituting the State for the parents. And there will still be need to produce submissiveness in the lower caste, lest it should rebel against the rich. This will involve a low level of culture, and will perhaps lead the rich to encourage breeding among black rather than white or yellow proletarians. The white race may thus gradually become a numerically small aristocracy, and be finally exterminated by a negro insurrection.

All this may be thought fantastic, in view of the fact that most white nations possess political democracy. I observe, however, that the democracy everywhere permits the school teaching to be such as furthers the interests of the rich; school teachers are dismissed for being communists, but never for being conservatives. I see no reason to suppose that this will change in the near future. And I think, for such reasons as I have been giving, that if our civilisation continues much longer to pursue the interests of the rich, it is doomed. It is because I do not desire the collapse of civilisation that I am a socialist.

If we have been right in what was said earlier, the family is likely to die out except in a privileged minority. Therefore if there ceases to be a privileged minority the family may be expected to die out almost completely. Biologically, this seems inevitable. The family is an institution which serves to protect children during their years of helplessness; with ants and bees the community undertakes this task, and there is no family. So, among men, if infant life comes to be safe apart from the protection of parents, family life will gradually disappear. This will make profound changes in men's emotional life, and a great divorce from the art and literature of all previous ages. It will diminish the differences between different people, since parents will no longer educate their children to reproduce their peculiarities. It will make sex-love less interesting and romantic; probably all love-poetry will come to be thought absurd. The romantic elements in human nature will have to find other outlets, such as art, science, politics. (To Disraeli politics was a romantic adventure.) I cannot but think that there will be a real loss in the emotional texture of life; but every increase of safety involves some such loss. Steamers are less romantic than sailing-ships; tax-collectors than highwaymen. Perhaps, in the end, safety will become wearisome, and men will become destructive from sheer boredom. But such possibilities are incalculable.

IV

The tendency of culture in our time is, and will probably continue to be, towards science and away from art and literature. This is due, of course, to the immense practical utility of science. There is a powerful literary tradition, which comes to us from the Renaissance, and is backed by social prestige: a 'gentleman' should know some Latin, but need not know how a steam-engine is made. The survival of this tradition, however, tends only to make 'gentlemen' less useful than other men. I think we may assume that, before very long, no one will be considered educated unless he knows something of science.

This is all to the good, but what is regrettable is that science seems to be winning its victories at the expense of an impoverishment of our culture in other directions. Art becomes more and more an affair of coteries and a few rich patrons: it is not felt by ordinary men to be important, as it was when it was associated with religion and public life. The money that built St Paul's might have been used to give our navy the victory over the Dutch, but in the time of Charles II St Paul's was thought more important. The emotional needs that were formerly satisfied in aesthetically admirable ways are now finding more and more trivial outlets: the dancing and dance-music of our time have, as a rule, no artistic value, except in the Russian ballet, which is imported from a less modern civilisation. I am afraid the decay of art is inevitable, and is connected with our more careful and utilitarian way of living as compared with our ancestors.

I imagine that a hundred years hence every fairly educated person will know a good deal of mathematics, a fair amount of biology, and a great deal about how to make machines. Education, except for the few, will become more and more what is called 'dynamic', i.e. will teach people to do rather than to think or feel. They will perform all sorts of tasks with extraordinary skill, but will be incapable of considering rationally whether the tasks are worth performing. There will probably be an official caste of thinkers and another of feelers, the former a development of the

Royal Society, the latter a federation of the Royal Academy and the Episcopate. The results obtained by the thinkers will be the property of the Government, and they will be revealed only to the War Office, Admiralty or Air Ministry, as the case may be. Perhaps the Health Ministry will be included, if, in time, it becomes part of its duties to spread disease in enemy countries. The Official Feelers will decide what emotions are to be propagated in schools, theatres, churches, etc., though it will be the business of the Official Thinkers to discover how the desired emotions are to be caused. In view of the cussedness of schoolchildren it will probably be thought desirable that the decisions of the Official Feelers also should be Government secrets. They will, however, be allowed to exhibit pictures or preach sermons which have already been sanctioned by the Board of Elder Censors.

The daily Press, presumably, will be killed by broadcasting. A certain number of weeklies may survive for the expression of minority opinions. But reading may come to be a rare practice, its place being taken by listening to the gramophone, or to whatever better invention takes its place. Similarly, writing will be replaced, in ordinary life, by the dictaphone.

If wars are eliminated and production is organised scientifically, it is probable that four hours' work a day will suffice to keep everybody in comfort. It will be an open question whether to work that amount and enjoy leisure, or to work more and enjoy luxuries; presumably some will choose one course, some the other. The hours of leisure will no doubt be spent by most people in dancing, watching football and going to the movies. Children will be no anxiety, since the State will care for them; illness will be very rare; old age will be postponed by rejuvenation till a short time before death. It will be a hedonist's paradise, in which almost everyone will find life so tedious as to be scarcely endurable.

In such a world it is to be feared that destructive impulses would become irresistible. R. L. Stevenson's Suicide Club might flourish in it; secret societies devoted to artistic murder might grow up. Life in the past has been kept serious by danger, and interesting by being serious. Without danger, if human nature remained unchanged, life would lose its savour and men would resort to all kinds of decadent vices in the hope of a little excitement.

Is this dilemma inescapable? Are the more sombre aspects of life essential to what is best in it? I do not think so. If human nature were unchangeable, as ignorant people still suppose it to be, the situation would indeed be hopeless. But we now know, thanks to psychologists and physiologists, that what passes as 'human nature' is at most one-tenth nature, the other nine-tenths being nurture. What is called human nature can be almost completely changed by changes in early education. And these changes could be such as to preserve sufficient seriousness in life without the spice of danger if thought and energy were devoted to that end. Two things are necessary for this purpose: the development of constructive impulses in the young, and opportunities for their existence in adult life.

Hitherto, defence and attack have provided most of what is serious in life. We defend ourselves against poverty, our children against an indifferent world, our country against national enemies; we attack, verbally or physically, those whom we regard as hostile or dangerous. But there are other sources of emotions which are capable of being quite as powerful. The emotions of aesthetic creation or scientific discovery may be as intense and absorbing as the most passionate love. And love itself, though it may be grasping and oppressive, is also capable of being creative. Given the right education, a very large percentage of mankind could find happiness in constructive activities, provided the right kind were available.

And this brings us to our second requisite. There must be scope for constructive initiative, not only for useful work ordered by a superior authority. There must be no barrier to intellectual or artistic creation, nor to human relations of a constructive kind, nor to the suggestion of ways in which human life might be improved. If all this is the case, and education is of the right kind, there will still be room for serious and strenuous living on the part of all those who feel the need of it. In that case, but in that case only, a community organised so as to eliminate the major evils of life as we know it might be stable, because it would be satisfactory to its more energetic members.

This is, I must confess, the matter upon which I feel that our civilisation is most likely to go wrong. There is need of much organisation, and where there must be so much, there is almost sure to be more than there ought to be. The harm that this will do will be the diminution of opportunities for individual effort. Vast organisations produce a sense of impotence in the individual, leading to a decay of effort. The danger can be averted if it is realised by administrators, but it is of a kind which most administrators are constitutionally incapable of realising. Into every tidy scheme for arranging the pattern of human life it is necessary to inject a certain dose of anarchism, enough to prevent immobility leading to decay, but not enough to bring about disruption. This is a delicate problem, not theoretically insoluble, but hardly likely to be solved in the rough-and-tumble of practical affairs.

BOOKS BY BERTRAND RUSSELL

1896 *German Social Democracy*

1897 *An Essay on the Foundations of Geometry* (Constable)

1900 *The Philosophy of Leibniz*

1903 *The Principles of Mathematics*

1910 *Philosophical Essays*

1912 *Problems of Philosophy* (Oxford U.P.)

1910–13 *Principia Mathematica* 3 vols (with A. N. Whitehead) (Cambridge U.P.)

1914 *Our Knowledge of the External World*

1916 *Justice in Wartime* (out of print)

1916 *Principles of Social Reconstruction*

1917 *Political Ideals*

1918 *Roads to Freedom*

1918 *Mysticism and Logic*

1919 *Introduction to Mathematical Philosophy*

1920 *The Practice and Theory of Bolshevism*

1921 *The Analysis of Mind*

1922 *The Problem of China*

1923 *Prospects of Industrial Civilization* (with Dora Russell)

1923 *The ABC of Atoms* (out of print)

1924 *Icarus or the Future of Science* (USA only)

1925 *The ABC of Relativity*

1925 *What I Believe*

1926 *On Education*

1927 *An Outline of Philosophy*

1927 *The Analysis of Matter*

1928 *Sceptical Essays*

1929 *Marriage and Morals*

1930 *The Conquest of Happiness*

1931 *The Scientific Outlook*

1932 *Education and the Social Order*

1934 *Freedom and Organization: 1814–1914*

1935 *In Praise of Idleness*

1935 *Religion and Science* (Oxford U.P.)

1936 *Which Way to Peace* (out of print)

1937 *The Amberley Papers* (with Patricia Russell)

1938 *Power*

1940 *An Inquiry into Meaning and Truth*

1945 *History of Western Philosophy*

1948 *Human Knowledge: Its Scope and Limits*

1949 *Authority and the Individual*

1950 *Unpopular Essays*

1951 *New Hopes for a Changing World*

1952 *The Impact of Science on Society*

1953 *The Good Citizen's Alphabet* (Gabberbochus)

1953 *Satan in the Suburbs*

1954 *Nightmares of Eminent Persons*

1954 *Human Society in Ethics and Politics*

1956 *Logic and Knowledge* (ed. by R. C. Marsh)

1956 *Portraits from Memory*

1957 *Why I Am Not a Christian* (ed. by Paul Edwards)

1957 *Understanding History and Other Essays* (USA only)

1958 *Vital Letters of Russell, Khrushchev and Dulles* (Macgibbon & Kee)

1958 *Bertrand Russell's Best* (ed. by Robert Egner)

1959 *Common Sense and Nuclear Warfare*

1959 *Wisdom of the West* (ed. by Paul Foulkes) (Macdonald)

1959 *My Philosophical Development*

1960 *Bertrand Russell Speaks his Mind* (USA only)

1961 *Fact and Fiction*

1961 *Has Man a Future?*

1961 *The Basic Writings of Bertrand Russell* (ed. by R. E. Egner & L. Dennon)

1963 *Unarmed Victory*

1967 *War Crimes in Vietnam*

1967 *The Archives of Bertrand Russell* (ed. by B. Feinberg, Continuum) (out of print)

1967 *Autobiography 1872–1914*

1968 *Autobiography 1914–1944*

1969 *Autobiography 1944–1967*

1969 *Dear Bertrand Russell . . .* (ed. by B. Feinberg and R. Kasrils)

1972 *The Collected Stories of Bertrand Russell* (ed. by B. Feinberg)

1973 *Bertrand Russell's America* (ed. by B. Feinberg and R. Kasrils)

1975 *Mortals and Others* (ed. by Harry Ruja)